T0278251

WORK, FIGHT, OR PLAY BALL

WILLIAM ECENBARGER

WORK, FIGHT, OR PLAY BALL

How Bethlehem Steel Helped Baseball's Stars Avoid World War I

TEMPLE UNIVERSITY PRESS
Philadelphia • Rome • Tokyo

TEMPLE UNIVERSITY PRESS
Philadelphia, Pennsylvania 19122
tupress.temple.edu

Published 2024

Text design by Kate Nichols

Library of Congress Cataloging-in-Publication Data

Names: Ecenbarger, William, author.
Title: Work, fight, or play ball : how Bethlehem Steel helped baseball's stars avoid World War I / William Ecenbarger.
Description: Philadelphia : Temple University Press, 2024. | Includes bibliographical references and index. | Summary: "This book describes the formation, operation, and reception of the Bethlehem Steel company's baseball leagues. It introduces the choices faced by baseball players in response to the Work or Fight order during World War I. It explores the intersections between baseball and the US War efforts at home and abroad"— Provided by publisher.
Identifiers: LCCN 2023020566 (print) | LCCN 2023020567 (ebook) | ISBN 9781439925171 (cloth) | ISBN 9781439925195 (pdf)
Subjects: LCSH: Bethlehem Steel League (Baseball league)—History. | United States. Army—Recruiting, enlistment, etc.—World War, 1914–1918. | Baseball—United States—History—20th century. | Baseball players—United States—History—20th century. | Baseball—Social aspects—United States—History—20th century. | World War, 1914–1918—United States—Influence.
Classification: LCC GV863.A1 E33 2024 (print) | LCC GV863.A1 (ebook) | DDC 796.3570973/0904—dc23/eng/20230828
LC record available at https://lccn.loc.gov/2023020566
LC ebook record available at https://lccn.loc.gov/2023020567

♾ The paper used in this publication meets the requirements of the American National Standard for Information Sciences—Permanence of Paper for Printed Library Materials, ANSI Z39.48–1992

Printed in the United States of America

9 8 7 6 5 4 3 2 1

To George W. Ecenbarger,

who played catch with me nearly every night,

explained the infield fly rule,

and often told me, "Football is checkers,

baseball is chess."

CONTENTS

WORK, FIGHT, OR PLAY BALL

PROLOGUE

In the early fall of 1918, Bethlehem Steel's plant at Lebanon, Pennsylvania, was flush with back orders from a nation gone to war. At the plant's baseball field, a large, moon-faced man with skinny legs stepped up to home plate. The left-hander gripped the forty-two-ounce bat all the way down at the handle, maybe even overlapping the handle a bit. He waved the bat back and forth over his shoulder in jerky motions as he awaited the pitch. His right foot was ready to lunge forward and plant itself in a line with second base as he whipped the bat around with all his strength. Then, George Herman "Babe" Ruth connected and sent the ball high into the bleached denim sky.

The next day, in Reading, Pennsylvania, not far from the Reading Steel Casting plant, a scowling right-handed hitter hefted a big-barreled bat similar to Ruth's and placed his five-foot-eleven, 175-pound frame well back in the batter's box. He opened his stance and took his weight off his front foot. The pitcher released the ball, and a half second later, Rogers Hornsby, taking into account the ball's height, speed, and trajectory, rifled a line drive into center field.

Around the same time of year, near the Harlan & Hollingsworth shipyard in Wilmington, Delaware, several thousand fans crowded into Harlan Field to watch another left-handed hitter. His feet were almost together, and a bat he called Black Betsy was just off his shoulder, almost horizontal to the ground. His fielder's glove was stuffed into his hip pocket. The first pitch came to him at perhaps ninety miles per hour, but Shoeless Joe Jackson easily connected, and the ball rocketed over the right-field fence.

What were Babe Ruth (undoubtedly the greatest baseball player ever), Rogers Hornsby (maybe the greatest right-handed hitter of all time, with a .358 lifetime average), and Shoeless Joe Jackson (whose career batting average of .356 is the third highest in history) doing at steel mills and shipyards in 1918?

Staying out of the war.

They were not alone.

1

THE PRETEND DOUGHBOYS

One and a half years earlier, on a baseball field in New York, there was an extraordinary, never-seen-before sight. A military band struck up a martial tune; out onto the outfield grass marched the New York Yankees in battle array, wearing their blue caps and white, numberless uniforms (it would be twelve more years until players had numbers on their backs). They shouldered bats as though they were rifles. An army drillmaster with a voice like a bronze gong shouted, "ONE! TWO! THREE! FOUR!" The men took regulation twenty-four-inch steps, more or less, at 120 steps per minute, more or less. "LEFT! RIGHT! LEFT! RIGHT!"

It was the Yankees' opening day, April 11, 1917, just one week after the U.S. Senate had declared war against Germany and entered the nation into World War I. Just as they would for another century, the Yankees were playing the Boston Red Sox. The venue was the Polo Grounds. The House That Ruth Built (Yankee Stadium) had not been built yet. Babe Ruth was on the field, but he was warming up in a Red Sox uniform, ready to pitch against the Yankees, whom he would hold to three measly singles.

Some sixteen thousand fans, fewer than half the Polo Grounds capacity, some with shoulders hunched against chilly air, watched as the Yankees went through their drills. "FORWARD MARCH! LEFT FACE! DOUBLE TIME!" Many eyebrows arched with surprise. The *New York Times* reported, "If anyone expected to see an awkward squad with the soldiers walking over each other's heels, he was completely fooled. The Yankees paced up and down, in and about, the ball yard just like a detachment of zouaves."

The ersatz soldiers headed out to the flagpole. "HALT!" They stood in company formation, neat and orderly, like the cots in a barracks. "PRESENT ARMS!" The Yankees lifted their bats out in front of them. Regulations call for triggers to be faced outward, but their "weapons" didn't have any triggers, only knobs, grips, and handles. The band members stood, lips poised on brass and reed. Then came "The Star-Spangled Banner." Pointed notes pierced the air as the flag was raised.

All around the horseshoe-shaped Polo Grounds, Old Glory fluttered from hundreds of flagpoles, and the grandstand uprights were swathed with patriotic bunting. The entire ballpark seemed to be upholstered. General Leonard Wood, a former army chief of staff, threw out the first ball.

About this same time, a few miles away, over in Brooklyn, the Dodgers opened their season against the Philadelphia Phillies of the National League before some eight thousand fans at Ebbets Field. The Dodgers, with American flags embroidered on the left side of their shirts, stood capless at attention in center field as some 350 naval reservists assisted in the raising of the flag while a navy band played "The Star-Spangled Banner."

At Shibe Park in Philadelphia, before facing the Washington Senators, the Athletics of the American League fell into ranks under the direction of army sergeant W. E. Smart and marched to the center-field flagpole. Then, they proceeded to execute a series of drill maneuvers toward home plate with, according to the

Philadelphia Inquirer, "the neatness and dispatch of regular soldiers." However, they shouldered neither bats nor rifles.

An hour later, in St. Louis, the Browns opened their 1917 season in Sportsman's Park against the Chicago White Sox, who showed up in new blue uniforms with white stripes and an American flag on the right sleeve. Players from both teams circled the ballpark, marching in groups of four. The White Sox had been drilling for weeks and, shouldering their bats, were far more impressive than the home-team players, who were empty-handed.

The following week, in Chicago, the White Sox opened their home season, and, again, the opponent was the St. Louis Browns. Most of the twenty-seven thousand fans were surprised to see their hometown heroes march out on the field wearing regular army khaki and this time shouldering real Springfield rifles. "Everywhere one looked, from scoreboard, along bleachers, pavilions and grand stand back again to the tall center field background," reported the *Chicago Tribune*, "it was one circle of red, white and blue. For an instant, there was a pause of surprise, then as the rooters recognized their idols they realized the transformation that had taken place since they last saw them. There was a roar which fairly drowned the band, which was trying to furnish a quickstep for the Sox to march by." There were six military bands, and the onlookers included seven thousand soldiers.

While the forces pushing the United States onto the battlefield were many, this particular tsunami of patriotism originated with one man. Tillinghast L'Hommedieu "Cap" Huston was a civil engineer with a military background who, along with beer baron Jacob Ruppert, had recently purchased the Yankees. Early in 1917, the United States had been quickly spurred to action when Germany resumed unrestricted submarine warfare—a move that, inevitably, would cost American ships and lives.

With war fast approaching, "preparedness" became a national obsession, and the baseball owners sought to offer an example of preparedness to the rest of America. Believing that Major League players should prepare not just for baseball but also for military service, Huston suggested that all teams institute military drills under army supervision as part of spring training. Moreover, the teams should drill before every game during the regular season. The War Department agreed to provide regular army drill instructors for each team.

Huston's idea was quickly and enthusiastically endorsed by Ban Johnson, the president of the American League, who saw benefits for the players and the soldiers. "The army is not going to let an opportunity like this pass by without getting some benefits in return for the drills," Johnson said. "Consequently, officers will be assigned to the teams [who] have more than a passing interest in the national game, and when the training period is over not only will the ball player be ready to step into the trenches, the drill sergeant will have absorbed a lot of inside baseball. Thus, it will come to pass that the ball players will know the whys and wherefores of 'hep, hep, hep' and the [Army] regulars will in due time learn that it won't do to sacrifice with two outs."

The drills were also a way for Major Leaguers to avoid being viewed as *slackers*—the fast-growing pejorative applied to men of draft age who were trying to avoid military service or otherwise not "doing their bit" in the war effort. And, finally, there was the pervasive belief, or at least hope, among the baseball moguls that in the event of a draft, the players would be immune so long as they participated in military instruction at their workplace. Thus, the games would continue—and the gate receipts would flow into the owners' pockets.

The Yankees held their spring training at Macon, Georgia, where the local army recruiter, Sergeant Smith Gibson, was assigned to drill the players for two hours every day. Thirty-two ball players showed up for the first drills on March 6. They were joined by Huston, manager Bill Donovan, the business manager, a coach, a groundskeeper, a local businessman, and eight sportswriters. One reporter declined to drill and was immediately derided as a slacker by the other attendees. The *New York World* reported that Huston was "as enthusiastic as a little boy playing with his first toy. The owner of the Yankees praised the boys for their fine showing and is looking forward to a good team of soldiers as well as a good team of ball players."

Meanwhile, out in Mineral Wells, Texas, where the Chicago White Sox opened spring training, the usual trade rumors, contract disputes, and rookie evaluations were overshadowed by shouldered bats and drilling under U.S. Army sergeant Walter Smiley. Four players, including future Hall of Famer Eddie Collins, were "promoted" to corporal to lead their teammates in what was jokingly called the "BBNG"—the Base Ball National Guard.

There were army drill instructors at seven of the eight American League teams; over in the National League, only the Boston Braves and the Brooklyn Dodgers invited army personnel to put their players through infantry drills. However, a few weeks into spring training, the Dodgers, the Detroit Tigers, and the Cleveland Indians discontinued the marching on grounds it was taking up too much baseball training time.

The opening of the 1917 Major League Baseball (MLB) season was overshadowed because five days earlier, Congress had approved President Woodrow Wilson's declaration of war on Germany. The United States had remained neutral for three years of World War I, but two months of submarine warfare had fanned the flames of anti-German sentiment. Then came the interception of a telegram from the German foreign secretary to Mexico, proposing a German-Mexican alliance to wage war against the United States. There was an immediate groundswell of support for getting American boys "over there," and "doing one's bit" on the home front became a sacred duty. There was a national consensus that everyone ought to be engaged in the war effort—and that those who were not were slackers. Inevitably, baseball became immersed in the cauldron, and club owners sought to make the world safe for baseball, walking the fine line between baseball doing its bit and preserving the 1917 season.

General John J. Pershing, commander of the American Expeditionary Forces, had a standing force of some 108,000 men, making it the seventeenth-largest army in the world—and a fraction of the country's actual manpower needs. Wilson expected one million young Americans to leap at the opportunity to enlist in the military for World War I, but only about seventy-three thousand volunteers signed up. Acting on the advice of Secretary of War Newton Baker, Wilson turned to conscription, rather than volunteer enlistments, to fill the huge manpower gap. On May 19, Congress passed the Selective Service Act of 1917, requiring the registration of all American men between the ages of twenty-one and thirty-one for the draft. The statute was carefully written to avoid the abuses of the Civil War draft, such as bounties, substitutions, and purchase of exemptions. However, the law did allow exemptions for dependency, religious objections to war, and, most significantly, as it would turn out for baseball, essential occupations.

The implementation of the draft was placed in the hands of some 4,600 local boards led by prominent citizens. Each board issued draft calls based on a national lottery and determined exemptions. On June 5, a nationwide Army Registration Day was held, with dramatic results. Some 9.5 million men consented to a marked abridgment of their freedom and fanned the flames of war fervor. MLB went out of its way to ensure that all players between twenty-one and thirty-one, composing most of its rosters, showed up on Registration Day. Eventually, some twenty-four million men would be registered, and three million of them would be inducted into military service.

National League president John Tener suggested to the team owners that there was "no obligation, either fixed or moral, that we should depart from our daily routine of business" of playing scheduled games on Registration Day. Joined by American League president Johnson, Tener asked that all sixteen Major League teams "co-operate heartily" with the registration by having "bands be engaged to play patriotic music." Rather than canceling games, the music would "convey public expression of the willingness on the part of major league baseball clubs to serve the country at this vital crisis of its history."

Nevertheless, there was considerable confusion and consternation over the military draft in the world of baseball. The draft law exempted men who had families dependent upon them, but local draft boards were given wide discretion in interpreting the law. Some boards, such as Ruth's, exempted all married men—setting off a nuptial avalanche in their communities. But not all draft boards agreed that married men without children should stay home just to keep their wives company—especially men who were earning as much as $7,000 a year (about $155,000 today), like Ruth. According to his biographer Leigh Montville, Ruth "said little about the war and seemed to follow along with whatever the other players were doing. They joined the Massachusetts Home Guard, the backup to the activated National Guard. He joined too. They drilled in close order in a team competition set up by league president Ban Johnson, an attempt to give the game a patriotic shine. The Babe drilled too."

On July 20, 1917, Secretary of War Baker, blindfolded, drew the first of some ten thousand draft lottery numbers from a bowl. Some seventeen hours later, a total of 1,374,000 men had been called up. Lawton "Whitey" Witt, a twenty-two-year-old shortstop with the Philadelphia Athletics, was the first active Major League player to be called up. One cynical sportswriter, noting that Witt was with the sad-sack, seventh-place Athletics, suggested that "playing with the Athletics should be sufficient cause for rejection."

Because of the threat of losing players to the draft, most minor leagues closed operations in 1917, but the American and National Leagues wanted to surge ahead with full schedules. Although some War Department brass feared that the baseball season would distract public attention from the war effort, President Wilson indicated a desire for a continued baseball season as a diversion from war. And so the teams kept playing, with the baseball magnates going to extraordinary lengths, even contortions, to avoid being labeled unpatriotic or, even worse, "slackers." They were walking a narrow path between patriotic diversion and opportunistic safe harbor and did their utmost to demonstrate publicly that the season's continuation was in the national interest. Baseball reinvented itself as a symbol of American engagement, with owners using their teams, games, and players to promote the war effort.

The owners were well aware that the concept of what it meant to be an American was being widely discussed—and contested. The Wilson administration and Congress rushed through a series of laws designed to suppress any public opposition to the war. A huge propaganda machine promoted America's military effort.

According to historian Patricia O'Toole, "Even the most casual expression of doubt about the war could trigger a beating by a mob, and the humiliation of being made to kiss the flag in public. Americans who declined to buy Liberty Bonds . . . sometimes awoke to find their homes streaked with yellow paint. Several churches of pacifist sects were set ablaze. Scores of men suspected of disloyalty were tarred and feathered, and a handful were lynched. Most of the violence was carried out in the dark by vigilantes who marched their victims to a spot outside the city limits, where the local police had no jurisdiction. Perpetrators who were apprehended were rarely tried, and those tried were rarely found guilty. Jurors hesitated to convict, afraid that they too would be accused of disloyalty and roughed up."

Few words were more defamatory than *slacker.* Federal agents conducted "slacker sweeps," some at MLB games, to ferret out draft dodgers. "Slacker lists" were published in newspapers. The word was so incendiary that, if used by prosecutors to describe a defendant, it was grounds for reversal of a conviction. So many men had their teeth extracted to disqualify them physically that the War Department issued a warning to dentists that they were liable to prosecution for aiding draft evasion.

And so the baseball owners offered free admission to servicemen. "Nothing further than a uniform of Uncle Sam, whether the wearer be a private or an officer, will be required to secure admittance," promised the Philadelphia Athletics. "The invitation also includes the National Guard and Civil War veterans." Military recruiting stations were established in Brooklyn's Ebbets Field and in the home fields of the Chicago Cubs and the Chicago White Sox. Johnson, the American League president, organized a series of appeals over the public address systems at the ballparks, urging fans to enlist.

Clark Griffith, owner of the Washington Senators, raised money to buy baseball equipment and subscriptions to *The Sporting News* and *Baseball Magazine* for the troops. Griffith's "Ball and Bat Fund" was designed to "give the American soldier the kind of punch he needed to knock out the Hun." General Pershing, commander of the American Expeditionary Forces, responded appreciatively: "The army executives from President Wilson down have been quick to see the value of baseball as recreation for those undergoing military drills." Wilson sent his own contribution and letter of support. Johnson raised money to send three thousand baseball kits overseas to U.S. soldiers. When actor Douglas Fairbanks opened a campaign to send baseball bats to servicemen, he called it the "next best thing to having a seat at the Polo Grounds."

Charles Comiskey's Chicago White Sox were especially fervent in their support of the war. There was a White Sox "patriotic button" showing a baseball and rifle crossed, a likeness of Comiskey himself, with a bullet on one side and a baseball on the other. When the White Sox showed up for the 1917 World Series, they wore uniforms with American flags on both sleeves and a star-spangled "SOX" logo on the front of the jersey. While all owners feared a shutdown of the season, none was more terrified than Comiskey, who had just assembled a championship-level team by spending heavily. His biggest deal was acquiring Shoeless Joe Jackson, one of the premier hitters of the day, from the Cleveland Indians, at a cost in players and cash of $74,000.

Huston, who was an army colonel serving in France, said that the American League players had become so proficient at drilling that they should be drilling others. He suggested that fans be formed into companies under the direction of the ballplayers. "I suggest that each club form a company of 150 fans," he said. "Make them members of the home guard and let the ball players drill them daily, giving annual passes to all those who attend regularly." But there was little enthusiasm for the idea on the home front.

In addition to manpower, the United States faced another urgent wartime need: Huge amounts of cash were required to build and sustain the war machine, and between 1917 and 1919, America would borrow some $37 billion. The vehicle for raising the money from the public was the Liberty bond program. The government whipped up public support for the war finance effort. Bond rallies were staged in New York and other big cities by the government and financial institutions. Slogans popped up across America— "LIBERTY BONDS OR GERMAN BONDAGE," "COME ACROSS OR THE KAISER WILL," "A BOND SLACKER IS A KAISER BACKER," and "LEND A HAND TO UNCLE SAM OR BEND A KNEE TO THE KAISER."

The purchase of Liberty bonds was portrayed as a way for average Americans to "do their bit" for the war. Ethnic groups were pitted against each other and encouraged to buy more bonds to prove their superior patriotism. By purchasing bonds, Americans were, in effect, lending their government money, and they would be repaid at some future date at a 4 percent interest rate.

MLB players and teams took part in Liberty bond drives. Christy Mathewson, star pitcher for the New York Giants, helped sell some $100,000 in bonds in a single day. Sometimes, games were interrupted in mid-inning to sell war bonds. A spirited bond campaign to "knock out the Kaiser" ran during the 1917 World Series.

In his 2010 book, *The Empire Strikes Out: How Baseball Sold U.S. Foreign Policy and Promoted the American Way Abroad*, Robert Elias says that baseball and the military became inextricably linked in 1917: "But while Woodrow Wilson campaigned promising to keep the United States out of World War I, he pushed the nation into the conflict after his 1916 reelection. In line with America's increasingly majestic visions of itself, Wilson claimed the nation was fighting to 'make the world safe for democracy.' Baseball would join this crusade in some intriguing ways."

The National League's Tener opined, "This is a war of democracy against bureaucracy. And baseball is the very watchword of democracy. No other sport or business or anything under heaven exerts the leveling influence baseball does." Charles Murphy, a former Chicago Cubs owner, chimed in, "What a pity Germany does not play baseball! If [it did] its people would never engage in a war of conquest."

According to *American Boy* magazine, "When Germany calculated whether to bring the U.S. into World War I, it ignored America's system of school athletics. It goes far beyond the ability—taught by playing baseball—of throwing a grenade far and accurate. Its well-organized and well-drilled teams provided a foundation for military training."

So not only did baseball court an association with the American war machine; the U.S. military also bought into the association and took confidence from the supposedly unique military training that baseball provided America's soldiers. The linkage that America and baseball's organizers mutually sought to establish became a two-way street of patriotism. At the sprawling Great Lakes Naval Station, the navy's boot camp in Illinois, some 150 games were played in a single day. The Young Men's Christian Association (YMCA) organized baseball leagues in France and sent baseball equipment to Americans in German prisoner-of-war camps. Yankees owner Huston declared, "Marksmanship was instinctive with our soldiers. [I]t was baseball that fine-tuned the soldier and his shooting eye." The War Department's Commission on Training Camp Activities adopted the slogan "Every American Soldier a baseball player."

Stars and Stripes, the daily American military newspaper, used baseball metaphors in reporting news of the war, with such headlines as "Uncle Sam Pinch Hitting on Western Front," "Huns Hit .000 Against Lorraine Hurlers," "Kaiser Calls Bench Warmers into Play," and "Yanks Nip Hun Rally in Belleau Woods." Recruitment posters pictured uniformed soldiers winding up to pitch with the caption, "That Arm. Your Country Needs It!" Sportswriter William Heyliger said that while American youths had a national sport with a moral code, "The German boy has no national sport, and code of fair play." When Italy was defeated at the November 1917 Battle of Caporetto, *Baseball Magazine* blamed it on that nation's "want of baseball." General Pershing claimed that "in grenade and bomb throwing, Americans become proficient in a few days drill. I attribute this to baseball."

Indeed, as the 1917 season opened, the War Department came out with a "baseball grenade" designed to take advantage of Americans' baseball skills. It was shaped like a regular baseball and designed to be delivered with the same motion as pitching a baseball.

Branding did not always match reality, and America's baseball-focused marketing rose to such prominence that outside military observers saw reason to pour some cold water on the company line. Several months later, a warning came from an Australian Army officer, Lieutenant Lester Elliott: "I hate to discourage you, but your professional baseball players will make bloomin' poor bombardiers, unless they go through a lot of training." Elliott made his comments after watching the Cleveland Indians toss the horsehide around the diamond: "I've been told that American baseball players expect to raise havoc against the Germans because of their training in baseball, but that training is all wrong. One of the training stunts for the [Australian] soldiers in the intensive camps in France requires that the bombers shall throw almost without a rest for two hours. When you consider that each bomb weighs from 7-1/2 to 9-1/2 pounds, rather heavier than the American baseball, you will see the difficulty facing Americans who throw their baseball with a snap and overhand." Elliott said that the best grenade motion was a sort of half bowling motion, as used in English cricket, adding, "Seldom do the throwers see their target."

Yet for the broader American public, baseball and the war effort went hand in hand. Elias says that religious organizations also did their part.

They had already used baseball to proselytize abroad, spread the American way, and bolster the U.S. military presence. In World War I, they launched a new burst of "muscular Christianity." The YMCA was enlisted to provide military sporting activities, and in September 1917, it helped select the athletic director for the American Expeditionary Forces in Europe. It organized intercompany and barracks baseball leagues, and when Americans were captured, it sent baseball equipment to German prisoner-of-war camps. Promoting military baseball was rationalized on several grounds. Since one couldn't "put thousands of red-blooded

American boys together without having an uncounted number of diamond battles," baseball's denial would have undermined morale—not to mention morals: Camp baseball would keep soldiers' minds off alcohol and women. Others believed that while baseball would help the armed forces, the military—by promoting the game among soldiers—would also help keep the game alive during the war.

Although many states and municipalities banned professional sports on Sundays, many places ignored the law so that the Major Leaguers could play exhibition and fund-raising games. Even those that did not sometimes had to bow to the baseball-military partnership. One such instance resulted in the arrests of two future Hall of Famers, John McGraw and Christy Mathewson, who in 1917 were managing, respectively, the New York Giants and the Cincinnati Reds. They agreed to reschedule a game to an earlier date to accommodate some 2,100 men who were shipping out to France the next day. The game was played on a Sunday, in violation of state law. Some thirty-four thousand fans paid to see the game, which also was a fund raiser for the troops. McGraw and Mathewson were arrested two days later. Ultimately, the judge who heard their case dismissed the charges and instead thanked the two managers "for lending their services to the patriotic cause."

Team owners weren't the only ones with a financial interest in continuing the 1917 season. F. C. Lane, editor of *Baseball Magazine*, prompted at least in part by the knowledge that canceling the baseball season would have a decidedly negative impact on his publication, jumped into the fray:

> Enthusiasm is a fine thing and patriotism a vital necessity. . . . War is a sober business demanding the full co-operations of all classes and types of industry. And war above most things needs the helpful co-operation, not the extermination of

> athletic sport. . . . No industry has shown a stronger desire to do something of material benefit to the nation than baseball.
>
> We cannot believe that the administration would wreck the national game, the peculiar institution beloved by the masses in order to supply a few hundred ill-equipped young men for industries of which they know little[,] where their work would be on a par with the most unskilled labor in the land.

Baseball Magazine and other sports publications fused flag-waving and advertising. Reach Athletic Goods were touted as being "as popular in the camps and rest-fields of France as on the baseball grounds of America."

The music industry did its part to win the hearts and minds of America. The day after America entered the war, George M. Cohan wrote the stirring and jingoistic "Over There." Harry Von Tilzer, composer of the classic "Take Me Out to the Ball Game," offered "Batter Up: Uncle Sam Is at the Plate," which was performed at baseball parks and other venues. Even before the war declaration, the sinking of the *Lusitania* and the attendant loss of American lives prompted such compositions as "When the *Lusitania* Went Down," "*Lusitania* Memorial Hymn," and "Remember the *Lusitania*." These and other war-tinged songs were performed by the popular singers of the day. President Wilson ordered that "The Star-Spangled Banner" be played at all military occasions. The movie industry sought to stoke anti-German zeal with such films as *The Kaiser, the Beast of Berlin* and *The Prussian Cur.*

Johnson went to Washington with a dramatic offer to take any war-related job, but his actual intent was to get some players from each team exempted from the military draft. He said that this exemption would keep the baseball season going, which, after all, was the hope of the White House.

In an effort to bolster Johnson's plan, Branch Rickey, president of the St. Louis Cardinals, suggested that the Major League owners turn over all of their profits from the upcoming 1918 season to the federal government:

> By opening their books to the government and giving every penny of profit to Uncle Sam, the magnates would plainly show that they desire the continuance of baseball from patriotic motives and not merely to save the dollars they have invested in the game. Such a stand could not but gain the sympathy of every right-thinking man for baseball.
>
> I believe President Johnson of the American League made a mistake when he took the first step toward obtaining exemption for ball players. For baseball men to seek exemption for the game's players places baseball in an undesirable light. Baseball should not make the first move. In such times as these, all business is subservient to the government. If baseball is such a business as to make its continuance necessary for the welfare of the nation as I believe it to be, baseball should rely on the government to make the first move toward the game's preservation.
>
> The government knows what baseball is, what it means to the country. The president finds time to attend games even in times of utmost stress. . . . The argument Mr. Johnson and his supporters have in mind is no doubt that 288 men, the number for which he asks exemption, mean nothing in an army of millions.
>
> This business whose life depends on the exemption of 288 men furnishes diversion relaxation and reading matter for practically the entire country through the daily games in the major cities of the nation. This argument is plausible enough, but it is wrong in principle if the men engaged in

> baseball desire the exemption of these 288 men to preserve their dollars and not for the good of the nation.

Even though he was thirty-six years old and had a wife and four children, and therefore was not liable for the draft, Rickey enlisted in the army and served in France with the Chemical Warfare Service, where he saw duty alongside Ty Cobb and Christy Mathewson.

As the season wound down in August, Johnson set up a $500 prize for the best-drilled team in the American League. There was an additional $100 prize for the winning army drillmaster. A board of regular army officers judged the competitions, which were held in four cities. The prize was awarded to the St. Louis Browns. The $500 was to be distributed "as the players decided." It was suggested that the players give the cash to the American Red Cross, but the players decided otherwise and pocketed the money.

By the end of the 1917 season, baseball owners were resigned to the reduced coverage of their game so that more war news could reach the public. This was no small matter, for in the days before television and radio coverage, newspapers were the sole source of information about games for anyone who was not at the ballpark to witness them. It would be another seven seasons before the first play-by-play broadcast on radio, and so baseball stories often included inning-by-inning, batter-by-batter summaries.

The troubled 1917 season ended with half of the sixteen Major League teams running deficits and eight of the twenty minor league teams disbanding. Only about forty Major League players had entered the military service, but by the end of 1917, seventy-six Major League players were in military uniforms. Baseball moguls were eying the 1918 season warily, as were the players.

Spirited pennant races and playoffs were not confined to the American and National Leagues during 1917. Steel mills and shipyards all over the nation were also fielding teams, using the best players among their workforces. By far the most prominent was the Bethlehem Steel League. It was good baseball, but it was about to get much, much better—due largely to the efforts of a remarkable American businessman whose boyhood had centered on music and poetry rather than on baseball.

2

THE FIRST CHARLES SCHWAB

Today, the name Charles Schwab immediately brings to mind stocks, bonds, and Wall Street. But a century ago, the name evoked images, with equal clarity, of blast furnaces, beams, and steel mills. Charles Michael Schwab, the industrialist, was no relation to Charles Robert Schwab, the financial executive, but he, too, was a giant in American economic history.

The industrialist Schwab began working as a day laborer in a steel mill at the age of seventeen; eighteen years later, he was the head of one of America's most important corporations and a personal acquaintance of Andrew Carnegie, William Vanderbilt, Chauncey Depew, J. P. Morgan, and other leading industrialists. His management skills made him a global hero at the end of World War I.

But he did poorly under the influence and affluence, spending extravagantly and building a seventy-five-room residence on the banks of the Hudson River that was in its time New York's most luxurious residence. He was a drinker and a gambler. These tendencies, plus some unwise investments and the Depression, left him bankrupt and in debt when he died in 1939.

Schwab was born in 1862 in Williamsburg, Pennsylvania, a tiny borough along the Juniata River near Altoona, where his father worked in a wool mill owned by his grandfather. Schwab showed an early aptitude not for business but for music. At the age of four, he was singing in a children's choir. At the age of eight, he was playing a small organ that his mother had purchased for him. Music resonated throughout the Schwab home. In plays in grade school and high school, he was the center of attention.

According to his biographer Robert Hessen: "Charlie excelled not only as a singer and a student, but also as a showman, even at this early age. Whenever the class put on a pageant, play or recital, he was usually the star. The future orator of the steel industry, the man who never passed up an opportunity to regale his colleagues and customers with jokes and anecdotes and who freely acknowledged his pleasure in 'playing the part of clown and entertainer for the edification of my delighted friends' made his debut at the age of seven when he won a poetry recital."

When Schwab was twelve, his family moved to another small Pennsylvania town, Loretto, some seventeen miles west of Altoona in what is now Cambria County. His father had been suffering from spells of fainting and dizziness, and a physician recommended a move to an area of higher elevation than Williamsburg.

Here, he went to a high school that was part of St. Francis College in Loretto. According to historian William S. Dietrich, "The schooling was sound but heavily laden with moral precepts of the Franciscan founders, notably poverty, chastity and obedience. The education took, but the moralizing didn't. In later life Charlie diligently and successfully avoided all three admonitions. He was first in his class, not through unalloyed intellectual capacity, but rather through a good mind and dogged determination."

One of Schwab's teachers gave this appraisal: "Charlie especially liked arithmetic. Generally, it was easy for him, though sometimes it wasn't. But if it wasn't, Charlie would never let on that he didn't know the answer. Instead, he'd go to the blackboard and mark away with might and main. And he wouldn't stop until he had solved the problem, or convinced us that he knew how to get the right answer. In all things, Charlie was a boy who never said, 'I don't know.' He went on the principle of 'pretend you know, and if you don't know, find out mighty quick.'"

At seventeen, Schwab left the family home and went to Pittsburgh, where, through a family connection, he got a job in nearby Braddock at a grocery and dry goods store. It didn't work out because Schwab was bored with being a clerk, but the store was right next to Carnegie's Edgar Thomson Works, and one of the store's customers was William R. Jones, a legendary figure in the steel industry who ran the mill. Jones often came to the store to buy cigars, and he soon noticed young Schwab's eyes aglow with intelligence not often found in young men. In a rising tide of repartee, the clerk and the customer raised pedantic fingers, flexed their wits, and cracked wise. Much of the talk centered on a mutual love of music. Schwab began performing on the piano at Jones's home and later taught the Jones children how to play. Finally, Jones offered Schwab a job in the mill as a surveyor in the engineering department at $25 a month. The eighteen-year-old Schwab reported for work on September 12, 1879.

Schwab moved up rapidly through the steel company's ranks, reading and studying metallurgy, accumulating information like a nest-building bird. He became a draftsman, and then chief draftsman. Jones rewarded him by making him his messenger to Carnegie himself. It was an important position in the days before businessmen could telephone each other. According to Dietrich, "Once when Carnegie was delayed, Schwab played Carnegie's parlor piano. When Carnegie came in, he stopped, but Carnegie urged him on. Carnegie loved music, particularly Scottish tunes and ballads, and asked if Schwab could play his favorites at a party three days hence. Schwab had no Scottish repertoire, but rehearsed the selected numbers and performed to Carnegie's delight. On the slippery climb up the corporate pole, you have to perform, but your performance has to be visible. Charlie Schwab was now under the eyes of the big guy."

In his personal life, Schwab married Emma Eurana Dinkey after a three-year courtship. She was called Rana and was the daughter of the owners of a boardinghouse in Braddock where Schwab had rented a room. Schwab's mother, a devout Catholic, opposed the union, and Rana, a Presbyterian, had no intention of converting to Catholicism. So, the wedding was held at the Dinkey home. Rana was two years older than Schwab, and throughout their fifty-five-year marriage, they called each other "old lady" and "old lad." They did not have children.

Schwab continued his steady rise at the Edgar Thomson Works, and in 1886, Carnegie, on the recommendation of Jones, made Schwab general superintendent of the Carnegie Phipps Homestead Works, seven miles from Pittsburgh on the Monongahela River. Carnegie had bought Homestead in 1883 and converted it from rail production to the formation of structural shapes. Schwab's salary shot up to $10,000 a year (the equivalent of nearly $300,000 today). Before Schwab took over his new duties, Carnegie sent him to Germany and France to study the more advanced steel mills there and bring their methods back to Pennsylvania. A British steelmaker visited Homestead in 1887 and was so impressed by the operation that he offered Schwab $50,000 to run a mill in Birmingham, England. Schwab declined because of a disagreement over the compensation that would be paid to assistants who would accompany him to Britain.

After Jones was killed in an explosion at the Edgar Thomson Works in 1889, Schwab asked Carnegie for Jones's job. Carnegie, with some reluctance because he wanted Schwab to continue to grow the Homestead operation, obliged. At the age of twenty-seven, Schwab became the general superintendent of the largest steelworks in the United States. Carnegie called Schwab back to Homestead in 1892 to quell one of the bloodiest strikes in American history. Gary Hoover, executive director of the American Business History Center, says that Schwab was better than most of his contemporaries in dealing with workers: "While throughout his career Schwab fought unionization like almost every other industrialist of the era, he also had a rapport with workers that most did not. He did not fear meeting directly with the union organizers and leaders of the workers in his efforts to settle labor issues. He talked to virtually every worker on the day and night shifts, knowing them by their first names. During this crisis [Homestead], Schwab lived at the plant and worked seventy-two-hour stretches, with only a few short naps. The man was tireless."

Carnegie believed that Schwab had a uniquely diverse background in the steel industry, and so in 1897, he made him president of the Carnegie Steel Company. Schwab quickly set about cutting costs and creating production incentives for workers. By 1900, Carnegie Steel turned a profit of $40 million—and Schwab, who held 6 percent of Carnegie's stock, was a rich man who enjoyed a personal relationship with Carnegie. By this time, Schwab also had earned a reputation as a superb orator, and in 1900, he was invited to be the guest speaker at a gathering of New York's premier business leaders: Vanderbilt, Morgan, and others from the railroad, oil, and banking industries. Dietrich describes Schwab's talk:

> Its theme was the virtues of industry consolidation. He envisioned an industrial behemoth, with enough volume to concentrate huge plants upon a single product; what Harvard Business School Professor Wickham Skinner would later term "the focused factory." After the speech, Morgan guided Schwab to the privacy of a window seat, where the two carried on an animated conversation for another half-hour.

> Morgan concluded by asking Schwab to visit his office. In that brief conversation, the world's first billion-dollar corporation, United States Steel, was conceived. With a rapidly accelerated gestation period, the birth of the elephantine infant was announced on March 3, 1901.

After Schwab secretly engineered the sale of Carnegie Steel to a group of investors headed by Morgan in 1901, he was promptly named president of the new U.S. Steel Corporation. His initial task was a challenge—melding U.S. Steel's 213 mills into a holding company. Schwab had been able to run Carnegie Steel without significant interference from Carnegie himself, but now he faced continuous monitoring from a board of directors. And Dietrich notes that there was an even bigger problem: corporate philosophy. Carnegie Steel had used cost advantages to chase market share, but U.S. Steel was already a behemoth by design and needed to focus on maximizing profits rather than on increasing industry share. This mind-set was embodied in a rival executive in the company, Judge Elbert H. Gary, former president of the second largest of the entities merged to compose U.S. Steel. "Gary didn't drink, smoke, gamble or tell off-color jokes," according to Dietrich. "Sober as a judge, he was the anti-Schwab. As chairman of the board's executive committee, he steadily reduced the content of Schwab's job until it was patently subordinate to his own."

Schwab didn't help matters when in 1902 he rented a yacht from banker Anthony Drexel and sailed all the way from New York to Monte Carlo, where he headed for the casinos. A reporter for the *New York Sun* learned of the escapade and wrote a story headlined, "SCHWAB BREAKS THE BANK." The lead paragraph read, "Charles M. Schwab, President of the United States Steel Corporation, who has been playing roulette very high here during the past few days, broke the bank this afternoon . . . [and] won 50,000 francs. He left the table amid great excitement and a large crowd followed him."

Fifty thousand francs in 1902 is the equivalent of some $1.6 million today.

Schwab had failed to take into account that while he had operated in relative anonymity as head of Carnegie Steel, he was now a national figure heading up the U.S. Steel giant. So, when Carnegie learned of the Monte Carlo incident, he was shocked and sternly chastised his longtime protégé. However, according to Daniel Alef in his 2008 book *Charles M. Schwab: King of Bethlehem Steel*, "Carnegie should have been more concerned about Schwab's other indiscretions—he had several mistresses and fathered one illegitimate baby with his sister-in-law's nurse. Schwab's wife, Rana, undoubtedly knew about her husband's escapades."

Morgan initially defended Schwab, but the U.S. Steel executive committee, headed by Schwab's pious archenemy, Gary, was out for blood. After a long leave of absence, Schwab resigned in August 1903. He had held the top job for only three years, but he was already on a new trajectory.

During his tenure at U.S. Steel, Schwab made a personal investment in a small eastern Pennsylvania firm, Bethlehem Steel. The company was well run and supplied the U.S. Navy with armor plate and gun forgings. But the profits of Bethlehem Steel in 1904 were about 1 percent of those of U.S. Steel. Schwab soon added to this venture the Harlan & Hollingsworth Shipbuilding Company in Wilmington, Delaware. In ensuing years, he added the Fore River Shipbuilding Company of Quincy, Massachusetts; the Maryland Steel plant at Sparrows Point, near Baltimore, Maryland; and the American Iron and Steel Manufacturing Company, which had plants in Lebanon, Pennsylvania, and Steelton, Pennsylvania. These shipyards and plants would field baseball teams during World War I.

At one point during all these transactions, Schwab's maneuvers came under criticism, and he was accused, unfairly, of fraud by some newspapers. There was a spate of negative publicity, with such headlines as "Schwab Guilty of Big Fraud," "Schwab a Wrecker," and "Death Grip of Schwab."

Schwab began his years at Bethlehem Steel with a bold declamation: "I intend to make Bethlehem the prize steel works, not only in the United States but in the entire world."

Five years earlier, the company had instituted a scientific management system that relied heavily on statistics and charts. Schwab dismissed its proponents as "slide rule men" and followed the management style that had succeeded at Carnegie Steel. According to Dietrich, Schwab "moved quickly to diversify the customer base away from the U.S. government . . . and began producing special steel alloys, large machine pumps, hydraulic presses and, most notably, open-hearth steel rails."

Schwab had become even wealthier at U.S. Steel, and in 1901, he built a $7 million, block-long, seventy-five-room mansion in New York. It included a swimming pool, gymnasium, and six elevators. Designed by French architect Maurice Hébert, it combined details from three French chateaux. Schwab called it Riverside, and it was the largest free-standing family dwelling in Manhattan. Charlie and Rana held Gatsby-esque parties and once paid Enrico Caruso, the Italian tenor, $10,000 for a one-night performance. But by 1905, Schwab realized that he could not run Bethlehem Steel from New York City. So, he closed Riverside, and he and Rana moved into a fifteen-room house in Bethlehem. Riverside went into a long hibernation. In 1935, Mayor Fiorello LaGuardia rejected an offer to make Riverside the official mayoral residence on the grounds that it was too lavish and elaborate. It was razed in 1948 and replaced by an apartment complex.

Schwab's gambling instincts weren't confined to casinos, and he took a major risk in 1905 that was, perhaps more than any other factor, the key to building Bethlehem Steel into a national business powerhouse.

Henry Gray, an Englishman, invented a new structural beam

called an H-beam (because of its shape) that he believed would be not only stronger but cheaper to produce than the widely used I-beam. Schwab decided to produce Gray's beam, which would come to be called a Bethlehem beam, but one obstacle loomed: He would need about $4.5 million to build a new plant to mass-produce the revolutionary product. Despite a financial panic in 1907, Schwab scraped together enough money to set up the new operation. Schwab even received money from Carnegie, a clear indication that the breach between the two men had dissolved. In fact, when Carnegie lay on his deathbed in 1919, he asked his secretary to bring him a photograph of Schwab; Carnegie looked at the image, smiled, and died.

Bethlehem began producing the beam in 1908, and it was an immediate success. In its 2003 special issue "Forging America: The Story of Bethlehem Steel," the *Allentown Morning Call* reported, "About 8,000 tons were ordered for the State Education Building in Albany, N.Y., and another 3,000 tons for a sugar refinery in Boston, but the coming-out party for Bethlehem's new beam was the headquarters for the Gimbel Brothers Department Store in New York. The 12,000-ton order, valued at $384,000 or the equivalent of $7.6 million today, was by no means going to make Bethlehem Steel's year, but it gave Schwab a showcase for his promising new beam, kicking off decades of dominance in the New York market."

Schwab had gambled and won. Alef says that the beam "revolutionized building construction. Schwab's H-beam made the age of the skyscraper possible." In testimony before Congress, Carnegie gave this assessment of his longtime protégé: "Mr. Schwab is a genius. I have never met his equal."

Soon after the outbreak of World War I in 1914, Schwab was summoned to London, where he met with three top British officials, including First Lord of the Admiralty Winston Churchill. Schwab came away with $135 million in orders (about $3.7 billion today), and not long after, Bethlehem Steel got an order for twenty submarines. This deal presented a problem because it would violate U.S. neutrality laws, but Schwab engineered a plan to get around this restriction by shipping the submarine components to Canada, where they would be assembled. Germany was outraged and offered to buy Bethlehem Steel for $10 million. The British countered with a $150 million offer. Schwab rejected both.

Bethlehem Steel had sixteen thousand workers in 1914. By 1917, when America entered the Great War and orders from the U.S. military and other Allied Powers exploded, the workforce swelled to thirty-five thousand, and Bethlehem Steel was the third-largest industry in America, topped only by U.S. Steel and Standard Oil of New Jersey. By the war's end in 1918, Bethlehem stock, which had sold for $7 a share in 1907, reached $700. Schwab, at the age of fifty-six, was one of America's wealthiest men.

A new federal agency, the Emergency Fleet Corporation (EFC), was established in 1917 to accelerate the construction of cargo and troop ships. The EFC faltered badly and could not meet the demands necessary to send one hundred thousand troops to France. The situation was desperate. If American troops could not arrive soon enough, the western front would be threatened with collapse. President Woodrow Wilson asked Schwab, whose company was the largest shipbuilder in the world, to take over the agency. Schwab initially demurred, but after constant pressure from Washington, he agreed to meet with Wilson himself in the Oval Office. After listening to the president's entreaties and flattery, Schwab agreed to take the job. But he asked Wilson, "Will you stand back of me?"

"To the last resources of the United States of America," Wilson replied.

Schwab took over and moved posthaste. He set up a headquarters in Philadelphia and recruited men he knew could perform. He streamlined paperwork, demanded that shipyard owners toe the line, and set up incentives for workers. He personally visited shipyards and talked to workers. Within three months, production doubled. "These events again put Charles Schwab in the spotlight, a miracle worker and wartime hero," according to business historian Hoover.

Biographer Hessen says that for Schwab's entire business career, he believed that his workers would respond to the same stimuli as he did—money and other tangible rewards: "Throughout his life, he gave his subordinates positive incentives, bonuses, and promotions, rather than threatening to fine or fire them if their efforts fell short." Early in his days at Bethlehem Steel, Schwab challenged a subordinate to reach a production goal by offering to pay off his mortgage if he succeeded; the man did and was mortgage-free in a few months. Schwab himself once described his strategy: "Do so much and you get so much; do more and you get more."

Schwab believed that a business could succeed only if its workers had a direct stake in that success. He set up an elaborate system of performance measuring to allocate these rewards.

In a brief, fawning history of Bethlehem Steel published in 1910, Arundel Cotter gives an example: "A Worker on shell castings, for instance, is paid 22 cents an hour and is given a job which should take five hours and on which his pay would be $1.10. If he got through the work in three hours, his pay would be $1.10." With this incentive, of course, this hypothetical worker would finish his shift in less time so he could start another and make more money.

Schwab was vigorously anti-union, and one deterrent he used was the creation of various forms of entertainment for the workers at his plants. These included choirs, social organizations, and athletic teams. The first big step toward his historic sports legacy came in 1911 with the formation of a company soccer team known as the Bethlehem Steel Football Club. Many of the plant workers were immigrants or the sons of immigrants from Europe, where soccer was a popular sport. Some soccer historians say that it was the most successful American soccer team in the first half of the twentieth century. Initially, men at the plant worked five days a week and practiced and played soccer on weekends, but the team joined the American Soccer League in 1922 and soon was playing before national audiences. With a $50,000 investment, Schwab built a soccer stadium and recruited star players from other professional teams. Bethlehem Steel disbanded the team in 1930 due to economic pressures, but not before it had won eight league championships, six American Cups, and five National Challenge Cups.

During World War I, Bethlehem Steel, through Schwab's planning and maneuvering, had a virtual monopoly in supplying America's wartime allies with munitions, and so in 1917, with company coffers bulging, Schwab turned to America's most popular sport and created a six-team baseball league to entertain his workers with what was then the national pastime. The *Allentown Democrat* reported, "Chas. M. Schwab has become a base hall [*sic*] magnate. He has commissioned Walter F. O'Keefe, of the Bethlehem Steel Co., to organize a league of six teams in order that the munition makers may enjoy the national game this year at the $35,000 base ball park Schwab has furnished in South Bethlehem, Pa."

Schwab gave these instructions to O'Keefe: "I want some good wholesome games that will furnish amusement and entertainment for the Bethlehem Steel Company's employees, and don't bother me about details of expense."

Schwab called the new adventure the Bethlehem Steel League (BSL), with teams at Pennsylvania steel plants in Bethlehem, Lebanon, and Steelton and shipyards in Wilmington, Delaware; Sparrows Point, Maryland; and Fore River, Massachusetts. At first, the players were all workers at the plants and shipyards—but that would soon change. Nothing in any of Schwab's biographies indicates that he was a baseball fan. He saw the league as a management tool rather than as a source of personal entertainment. If the workers were predictably compensated for their work, invested in intramural rivalries, and entertained by their workplace's unusual perk made possible by their understanding owner, they would be less likely to organize themselves for union demands.

In its first year, the league was strictly a low-key operation, drawing its players from the body of regular plant workers. As the season progressed, a few semiprofessional players and former Major Leaguers joined the BSL teams. Schwab saw to it that rivalries developed between the plants to motivate high attendance. Each plant spruced up its field and made accommodations for more spectators. Games were scheduled on Fridays, Saturdays, or Sundays so players would lose only one day of work.

The 1917 BSL season opened on June 9 in Quincy, Massachusetts, where Sparrows Point defeated Fore River, 5–1. Nelson Way, who had briefly pitched for the New York Giants, held the home team to four hits. Way, a Yale graduate, was a controversial figure. After he was released by the Giants, he said that the national pastime was "low brow" and suggested that if one went into Major League Baseball (MLB) with a college education, one would come out without it.

Umpiring was a frequent problem for the new league. In a game between Lebanon and Sparrows Point, Lebanon, the visiting team, loaded the bases with two outs. The batter hit a double, scoring three runs, but the umpire ruled that one runner had failed to touch second base and was therefore out. Only one run was scored. The umpire was a member of the Sparrows Point team. The *Lebanon Evening Report* complained, "This incident shows the need for neutral umpiring at all baseball games, especially in an organization like the BSL. It is always evident that the home umpire is favorable to the local team. It is hoped that a ruling of this kind will be made for the next season and a square deal be insured all teams." Out-of-town umpires were used for most games in the 1918 season.

Bethlehem and Lebanon tied for the league lead, with 9–2 records. Sparrows Point finished at 6–3; Fore River, 4–6; Steelton, 3–7; and Wilmington, 1–9. In a playoff at neutral Steelton on September 2, Lebanon defeated Bethlehem 3–2 to win the BSL pennant. Some 3,500 fans watched as Bill Ritter, who had pitched for the Phillies and the Giants before retiring in 1916, held Bethlehem to four hits. Two National League umpires were brought in for the game. The next day, the *Lebanon Evening Report* gushed, "Hail the champions! The gonfalon . . . shall float from the pole in deep center at Third and Green streets under Old Glory, and on one corner of that grand old baseball rag might be sewed the initial of the man who made this thing possible, big Bill Ritter."

Before the 1918 BSL season opened, Schwab left for his federal shipyard post. He turned the company operations over to Eugene G. Grace, who had joined Bethlehem Steel in 1899 as a fifteen-cents-an-hour electric crane operator. Grace's abilities soon came to the attention of Schwab, who sent him to Cuba in 1906 to solve a problem with the company's principal source of iron ore. Grace performed well and rose quickly to become the president of Bethlehem Steel in 1913. When Schwab left to run the shipyard agency, Grace became, in effect, the company's CEO, a role he would continue to fill until ill health forced him to retire in 1957. Historian Dietrich notes that this shift was a reversal of roles for Schwab, who had gone from running the company Carnegie owned to owning the company Grace ran.

Schwab moved on to supervise the nation's shipyards, and soon they, too, would have a baseball league of their own.

Schwab himself began a long decline fueled by extravagance. He traveled in a $100,000 private rail car, got into high-stakes gambling, had a series of extramarital affairs, and kept a personal staff of twenty-seven. He built a forty-four-room estate on one thousand acres in Loretto, Pennsylvania, the town that was his boyhood home. There, the chickens were roosted in replicas of French cottages, and the estate boasted a nine-hole golf course, hanging gardens, and a twenty-six-room guesthouse. Called Immergrun ("Evergreen" in English), it cost $3 million. The combination of unchecked spending and the Great Depression left Schwab $300,000 in debt when he died in 1939.

But back in 1918, Schwab left the BSL in sure hands. Not only was Grace a baseball fan; he had been a star and captain of the Lehigh University team. One day at Lehigh, Grace got a chance to play an exhibition game against the Boston Braves, and he hit a home run; he was offered a contract by the Braves, but he turned it down to go to work for Bethlehem.

3

WORK OR FIGHT

By the time the 1918 Major League Baseball (MLB) season opened, the win-the-war hysteria had been injected into every aspect of life in America. The tone was set at the White House, where President Woodrow Wilson said, "To fight you must be brutal and ruthless. Force to the utmost! Force without stint or limit. The righteous and triumphant Force which shall make Right the law of the world . . . and cast every selfish dominion down in the dust." Across the nation, steel mills, shipyards, and coal mines worked round-the-clock.

Baseball was not exempt from this fervor, and the question foremost on club owners' minds was not whether they would be affected but rather how extensive the wreckage would be. They pressed for a complete 154-game schedule for the coming season with full rosters of draft-exempt players. In return, the magnates tried to show their commitment to the war effort. They played charity exhibition games and purchased Liberty bonds. The teams continued their pregame military drills. On opening day in Washington, the British and the French flags joined the Stars and Stripes in honor of the nation's new allies. President Wilson was busy with war matters, but Assistant Secretary of the Navy Franklin D. Roosevelt marched onto the field with the Senator players. Nevertheless, as Americans were dying in Europe, many at home were wondering why baseball players should be exempt from the fray.

Then came a figurative bombshell from Europe. Colonel Cap Huston, the Yankees part-owner who had been serving in France since the summer of 1917, had been following the owners' antics in newspapers and did not like what he was reading. In response, he composed a two-thousand-word article published in several New York newspapers that read in part:

> Everybody but the men managing baseball sees the immediate serious situation to which America is exposed. If they don't wake up from their stupor and put the national game in its rightful place in the front ranks of all patriotic movements, events combined with public opinion will force them out and put others more alert in their places. This is no time to "four flush" with the public. Beware of trifling with the situation. It's loaded.
>
> The small percentage of the proceeds of the [1917] World Series donated was ridiculous and really insulting to the Nation. At least 25 percent should go for patriotic purposes. This would tend to take away the bad taste always left by this annual baseball financial orgy, which is fast becoming a menace to the life of the national game, for if not abated, some fatal scandal is bound to occur sooner or later. There have already been some close shaves.
>
> The lack of patriotism shown in baseball circles is a disgrace. Very few big league players volunteered. . . . Not a person connected with the business end of baseball has volunteered. Ye gods, what a mortifying and shameful spectacle!

Any opposition from the owners was muted. Only Charles Ebbets, owner of the Brooklyn Dodgers, spoke forcefully: "I do not think that Huston's remarks on that score were in good taste or that they were backed by any definite information. We certainly did as well as we could last year. We intend to do better this season—that is, if some of us do not go bankrupt." But Huston found allies in the nation's newspapers, including the *Washington Times*, which reported, "The magnates continued to trudge along in their blindness until last week when the bomb landed in their camp. It caught them unprepared." The *New York Tribune* advised, "No one can question the patriotism of Ban Johnson or his colleagues. They have done many services which have proven their loyalty. But they seem to have neglected the really great things. If they are wise they will heed his admonitions. He at least has proved himself qualified to lead."

A week later, the magnates found themselves embroiled in more controversy, this time over the advent of daylight saving time (DST), which Congress had adopted on March 9 as a means to have more daylight during working hours. Other combatants, including Germany, had already shifted to DST for the same reason. Baseball owners saw an opportunity for more dollars here and moved to seize it. Games usually started around 3:00 P.M. and became more difficult to play as the sun went down. Often, games were called because of darkness. Night games under lights would not come to baseball until 1935. Therefore, it seemed that the extra hour of daylight would be good for baseball. Nevertheless, some of the owners reasoned that if they started the games at 4:00 P.M., they would still have the same amount of daylight as before—but they would be very likely to increase gate receipts and profits with the later start.

The magnates found themselves labeled that lowliest of all words—*slackers*. Charles L. Pack, president of the National War Garden Commission, fumed, "Slackers of the worst type is the brand placed upon baseball team owners or managers who plan to move down the scheduled time of starting games this summer." Sportswriters were irate, none more than I. E. Sanborn of the *Chicago Tribune*, whose patriotic blood came to a boil: "The professional baseball league club owner that endeavors to profit by the daylight saving law deserves the name of slacker and the treatment accorded to that class of American citizen." Reluctantly, the owners backed down.

More bad news for the owners came on May 11, when the Bethlehem Steel League (BSL) and another Schwab-related circuit—the Delaware River Shipbuilding League (DRSL)—opened their 1918 seasons.

To be sure, other industrial baseball leagues played from coast to coast, and they were steadily recruiting and signing major and minor league players. Indeed, Bethlehem Steel had a four-team league in California with teams from shipyards in San Francisco, Alameda, Hunters Point, and Potrero. Other shipyard leagues played in New York, Seattle, and the Gulf Coast states. The Duluth team in the Head of the Lakes–Mesaba Industrial League, composed of mining, steel mill, and shipyard teams in Minnesota, sent telegrams to Walter Johnson, Ty Cobb, and George Sisler, asking them to join the teams and work in a shipyard or steel mill, but all three players declined. Other steel mill and shipyard teams courted Honus Wagner, the superstar Pirates shortstop, but he also declined. However, none of these circuits drew as many Major Leaguers as the two that bore the unmistakable imprint of Charles Schwab.

BETHLEHEM STEEL LEAGUE

Bethlehem (Pennsylvania)
Fore River (Quincy, Massachusetts)
Lebanon (Pennsylvania)
Sparrows Point (Baltimore)
Steelton (Pennsylvania)
Wilmington (Delaware)

DELAWARE RIVER SHIPBUILDING LEAGUE

Chester Ship (Chester, Pennsylvania)
Harlan & Hollingsworth (Wilmington, Delaware)
Hog Island (Philadelphia, Pennsylvania)
Merchant Ship (Bristol, Pennsylvania)
New York Ship (Camden, New Jersey)
Pusey & Jones* (Wilmington)
Sun Ship (Chester, Pennsylvania)
Traylor Ship (Cornwells, Pennsylvania)

* Replaced League Island Navy Yard after two games

Baseball executives were still smarting from the recent Federal League mutiny in which the Federal League of Base Ball Clubs operated as a third Major League, siphoning off talent from the American and National circuits in 1914 and 1915. *Baseball Magazine* reported:

> One disagreeable feature made itself manifest during May—what looked almost like a second Federal League, fostered and developed under the wing of the Government . . . a new league of steel, shipbuilding, and munition plants, with the players mostly well-known stars of the present or the past. There was a gasp of surprise when the list of players gathered by the steel plants was given out. . . . It was frankly asserted [by Major League owners] that agents of the steel plants were gathering big league stars, promising them fat salaries, nominal positions in the plants, with nothing to do but play ball, and at the same time pointing out that munition workers wouldn't have to go to the trenches.

The first BSL game pitted defending champion Lebanon steel mill against Harlan & Hollingsworth in Wilmington, Delaware.

The DRSL opener saw Bristol against Harlan & Hollingsworth. The opening rosters for both leagues were populated by semiprofessional and college ballplayers, with one exception. On April 22, veteran left-handed pitcher Eddie Plank, who had retired from the St. Louis Browns in 1917, agreed to pitch for Steelton in the BSL. But Plank, a future Hall of Fame member, was forty-two and did not need to evade the draft. The Browns had traded Plank to the Yankees, but he refused to sign a contract. He had a farm near Gettysburg, Pennsylvania, which was only forty miles from Steelton. Plank also had recently opened an automobile repair shop near Steelton. This arrangement allowed him to manage his affairs at home during the week and play for Steelton on weekends. Throughout his career, Plank was criticized for his pitching style, which involved long gaps between pitches when he adjusted his cap, asked for a new sign, and stared at a base runner. Plank ignored the barbs and won 326 Major League games; only ten other pitchers ever won more games.

Plank's defection to the steel league drew little attention outside central Pennsylvania, but the next Major Leaguer to jump to the BSL created a national frenzy. Joseph Jefferson Jackson, arguably the greatest natural hitter in the history of baseball, had a very limited education; by the time he was thirteen, he was working twelve-hour shifts in a textile mill in Greenville, South Carolina. But he was a standout on the company's baseball team, and at the age of eighteen, he signed a $75-a-month contract with the Greenville Spinners, which had just been formed to play in the Class D South Carolina League. During one of these early games, Jackson experienced blisters, and so he removed his cleats; a fan who noticed that he was playing in his socks heckled, "You shoeless son of a gun!" From that day forward, he was known as Shoeless Joe Jackson.

By 1918, Jackson had completed seven Major League seasons—first in Philadelphia, then in Cleveland, and then with the Chicago

White Sox—with a lifetime batting average of .352. Jackson was profiled, prophetically as it turned out, in *Baseball Magazine*: "The oddest character in baseball today is that brilliant but eccentric genius, Joe Jackson. . . . To sum up his talents is merely to describe those qualities which should round out and complete the ideal player. In Jackson, nature combined the greatest gifts any one ball player has ever possessed but she denied him the heritage of early advantages and that well balanced judgement [*sic*] so essential to the full development of his extraordinary powers."

According to Donald Gropman, author of *Say It Ain't So, Joe!*, Jackson had tried to enlist in the army in 1917 but was dissuaded by his wife, Katie, who reasoned that three of his brothers had already volunteered and that he was the sole remaining support for her, his mother, a younger brother, and a sister. His hometown draft board in Greenville, South Carolina, had obligingly classified him as Class 4, meaning that he was deferred. But as the war heated up and General John J. Pershing demanded more troops, the board reclassified Jackson as 1-A. A physical exam found him "100 percent sound," and he was notified that he would be inducted into the army between May 25 and June 1.

Clarence "Pants" Rowland, White Sox manager, was dumbfounded. He had assumed that Jackson's marital status would protect him, and he was loathe to lose his best hitter. After seventeen games, Jackson was hitting .354. Perhaps it was a mistake, Rowland thought, fingers crossed. After all, other Joe Jacksons were listed in the Greenville telephone directory. But the board confirmed that it wanted Shoeless Joe. As it happened, the White Sox had just finished a series in Philadelphia against the Athletics. When the team entrained for Cleveland the next day, Jackson was not on board. He announced that he had taken a job as a painter with the Harlan & Hollingsworth Shipbuilding Company, a subsidiary of Bethlehem Steel, in Wilmington, Delaware. After talking to Jackson by telephone, Rowland said that he joined the shipyard because he believed that he was "doing the right thing . . . to protect his family."

But Jackson's move to the shipyard drew heavy criticism from newspapers and baseball officialdom. Other Major Leaguers would take jobs in shipyards and steel mills, but Jackson was the first and so far the best known, and so he became the poster boy for "shipyard slackers."

Articles claimed that the players were given sinecures as "painter's assistants" whose jobs consisted of carrying two cans of paint to real workers and then practicing and playing baseball the rest of the day. The BSL and the DRSL were called "safe shelter leagues," "paint and putty leagues," and "Schwab leagues."

The *Chicago Tribune* published an editorial noting that Jackson was "a man of unusual physical development, and presumably would make an excellent fighting man, but it appears that Mr. Jackson would prefer not to fight." A *Tribune* columnist was harsher: "The fighting blood of the Jacksons is not as red as it used to be in the days of Old Stonewall and Old Hickory, for General Joe of the White Sox has fled to the refuge of a shipyard."

Ban Johnson leaped into the one-sided battle: "The American League does not desire to impugn the motives of the players who have gone into this work. Some of them are patriotic. But if there are any of them in class 1–A, I hope Provost Marshal General [Enoch] Crowder yanks them from the shipyards and steel works by the coat collar, and places them in cantonments to prepare for future events on the western front."

When two of Jackson's friends on the White Sox, pitcher Lefty Williams and catcher Byrd Lynn, joined him in the shipyard, newspapers widely blamed Jackson. White Sox owner Charles Comiskey hinted that Jackson, Williams, and Byrd might not be welcomed back to the team when the war ended: "There is no room on my club for players who wish to evade the army draft by entering the employ of shipbuilders." But what really tormented

Comiskey, of course, was that Shoeless Joe was not playing for the White Sox. The *Chicago Tribune* noted that because the team's home uniforms were at the cleaners, the White Sox were playing home games in their road uniforms. Then it suggested facetiously, "Comiskey ordered the uniforms disinfected for fear some of the Schwab germs which infected Jackson, Williams, and Lynn might have crept into the other players' suits."

The defections of Williams and Byrd inspired a sarcastic poem in *The Sporting News*:

Two more bold, fearless ath-a-letes of note
Have gone to captivate the Kaiser's goat
And save the world from Hun autocracy
By smearing gobs of paint upon a boat.
Men fought with spear and war clubs long ago,
Then came the guns which laid the foreman low;
And now the athlete takes his pot in hand
And swings his trusty paint brush on the foe.

The Sporting News was a dependable advocate of owners' interests, and it ran editorials about the "Jackson case": "At a time of every man doing his patriotic duty," Jackson was "cleverly seeking exemption when by all rights . . . he should be in an Army or Navy training camp." As more and more players left for wartime jobs, they were accused of "taking the Joe Jackson route." In *From the Dugouts to the Trenches*, Jim Leeke says, "All season long, in any newspaper article listing ballplayers who had landed jobs in shipyards or steel plants, Jackson's name inevitably came first."

When the criticism was read to Jackson (he was illiterate), he was embittered and pointed to his wife in Savannah, his widowed mother and two siblings in Greenville, and his three brothers in uniform in France as evidence that he was needed at home and that the Jackson family was doing more than its fair share for the war effort. "It makes no difference when the war ends," he declared. "I shall not attempt to go back to ball playing to make a living. I intend to make my home here and follow the trade of shipbuilding." Sadly for Jackson, he did not follow through on that promise. Rather, he returned to the White Sox, which infamously became known as the Black Sox in 1919 after Jackson and seven other Chicago players were accused of deliberately losing the World Series in exchange for payments from a gambling syndicate. All eight players were banned from baseball for life.

A few sportswriters rose to Jackson's defense. "I can't understand why Jackson was placed in Class One-A," wrote one. "There are many stars of the big leagues who are married and have many times the amount of wealth Joe possesses who are in Class Four." Another defender was Alfred von Kolnitz, a White Sox infielder who enlisted in 1916 and soon rose to the rank of army major. He said that Jackson should be exempt: "There are thousands of men walking the streets in civilian clothes with exemption papers in their pockets with far less claims than Joe." No one mentioned Babe Ruth, whose marriage deferment was still intact and who was playing baseball every day for the Red Sox.

For what it's worth, Jackson's duties at the shipyard went well beyond the cushy lifestyle imagined by his detractors. A week after he arrived in Wilmington, the *Evening News* reported, Jackson was "in charge of a bolting up gang on a ship that is to be floated at the Harlan plant this week. When some one of the gang falters, it has been no unusual thing to see Jackson pitch in and do the same physical work that the others are doing." However, the article went on to suggest, somewhat dubiously, "But it is his 'noodle' that the shipyard bosses want most of all. The plant is constantly extending its capacity and the yard needs men of brains such as Jackson possesses. If he didn't have the brains he could not have won the fame he did in the big league." In an article published in *Delaware History* titled "Slugger or Slacker? Shoeless Joe

Jackson and Baseball in Wilmington, 1918," Peter T. Dalleo and J. Vincent Watchorn III say that Jackson worked five eight-hour days plus a four-hour shift on Saturday before practicing baseball.

Why was Jackson targeted for so much degradation while Ruth and many others continued profitable careers playing Major League ball? One reason was that at this time, Ruth was not as well known in the baseball world as Jackson. Kelly Boyer Sagert, a Jackson biographer, speculates, "It may . . . merely have been a difference in civic attitudes between Boston or New York and Chicago. Anti-war sentiment and conscientious objection was more common in the East Coast cities than in the Midwest, where the agitation for the United States' involvement had been active from early in the conflict. As a 'home town hero' of Chicago, Jackson's demurring from the draft may well have been perceived as a betrayal of local values."

Jackson biographer David L. Fleitz notes that many Major Leaguers who joined the military were far from the battlefields: "Many of them joined 'special services' units and played far more baseball than Jackson did. However, because Joe was the first prominent player to decline service in the military at a time when patriotism was running at a fever pitch, Joe was the one who took the greatest amount of criticism from the sportswriters."

OVER HERE. Localized draft boards were instituted with the intention of being sensitive to local conditions. The result, however, was an inconsistent hodge-podge of policies and prejudices. One Georgia board exempted 526 of 815 white men but only 6 of 202 black men. The definition of *dependency* varied widely from board to board. Some boards, like Ruth's, simply exempted all married men, igniting a nuptial hailstorm. Others, like Jackson's, dug deeper and looked at possible support from relatives, the wife's chances of employment, and other factors. Resentment grew in some communities because of this snooping. Poor men were often singled out because they were considered less likely to possess the skills needed for the war effort on the home front. Governor Martin Brumbaugh of Pennsylvania, a Republican, infuriated Democrats by placing GOP loyalists on boards in the state's heavily Democratic communities. Around the nation, state induction rates varied from 6 percent to 38 percent. After his son-in-law was denied an exemption, Senator Hiram Johnson complained that the draft was "being administered in such fashion as to make it unfair, unequal, partial, and discriminatory."

Another major prize for the industrial leagues was Charles Albert "Chief" Bender, who had recently retired from the Phillies but was being courted by several other Major League teams, including the Yankees. Instead, Bender opted to go to work at the huge Hog Island shipyard in Philadelphia. "Baseball is a secondary consideration with me," he explained, "and while I realize that the fellows who are doing their bit [for the war] need amusement . . . I also realize that we need ships and all the men we can get to build them." Bender had just turned thirty-four, so he was out of the draft for the time being. His younger brother, Fred, was serving with the army in France.

In a Hall of Fame career, Bender helped the Philadelphia Athletics win three World Series. He pitched three complete games in the 1911 World Series. He won 212 Major League games and lost only 127, for a winning percentage of .625, and had a career earned run average of 2.46. Connie Mack, who managed him in the glory years, said that he would want Bender on the mound "if I had a pennant or world's championship hinging upon the outcome of one game."

Despite these credentials, Bender faced unremitting, overt racism throughout his career. While he was on the mound, opposing players in the dugout, so-called bench jockeys, would try to rattle him with racist "war whoops." Bender was an Ojibwa who had been born on the White Earth Reservation in northern Minnesota. During his playing years, he resented the nickname "Chief," saying, "I do not want my name to be presented to the public as an Indian, but as a pitcher." He did not make it into the Hall of Fame until 1953, thirty-five years after he retired. When he died the following year, *The Sporting News* headlined his obituary, "Chief Bender Answers Call to Happy Hunting Grounds."

"There is a limit to how long a man can carry the burden of race on his shoulders," writes his biographer Tom Swift. "The institutions and mores of the day, white-related and controlled, had forced Charles Bender to straddle a blunt color line. He knew two different worlds but didn't sit comfortably in either one."

There is every indication that Bender worked hard at his job as a riveter, putting in fourteen-hour days at Hog Island, which at the time was the largest shipyard in the world. He made his diamond debut for Hog Island on May 15, pitching three scoreless innings in relief against Harlan. Watching from the bleachers was Jackson, who would begin playing for Harlan the next weekend.

The next bombshell for MLB came from Washington on May 18 in reaction to events in Europe. The Russian Revolution had led to an end to hostilities on the eastern front and freed German troops to launch a spring offense in France. General Crowder, who headed the Selective Service operation, issued what became known as the "Work-or-Fight Order," which was designed to increase American military manpower. In essence, draft-age men who were engaged in nonessential work could be drafted into the army, beginning on July 1. Crowder explained that the order was aimed at "sturdy idlers and loafers standing at the street corners and contemplating placidly their own immunity." War-related work included steel-making, munitions, ship construction, and farming. There was no manpower shortage in any of these fields, but the intent was to prevent able-bodied men from languishing in flippant, superficial pursuits while their contemporaries were on the battlefield. Among the nonessential pursuits that would not earn a draft exemption were "persons engaged and occupied in and in connection with games, sports, and amusements." However, there was an exemption for theatrical performers, such as actors, singers, and musicians, because they provided "essential recreation." There was no mention of baseball players among the exempt professions.

The Work-or-Fight Order inspired local draft boards to demonstrate their patriotism, and many ballplayers who had thought themselves immune to military duty suddenly found themselves reclassified and about to be drafted. The more thoughtful fans began wondering why there weren't more ballplayers "over there."

Ban Johnson reacted swiftly to the Work-or-Fight Order, pledging baseball's outward support: "If I had my way, I would close every theatre, baseball park, and every other place of recreation in the country. I would make the people realize that we are in the most terrible war in the history of the world. Let us all go to war and buckle in, and fight to the limit." But then he added, "I don't believe the government has any intentions of wiping out baseball, but I don't care if they do."

It appeared that the 1918 MLB season would end on July 1. Roughly four in every five players were of draft age. Nevertheless, the baseball magnates held a faint hope that their season would survive. Many fans were choosing to spend their disposable income on Liberty bonds rather than on baseball tickets, and profits were way down. Red Sox owner Harry Frazee insisted, "If the proposition were put up to the fighting men themselves, they would vote 1,000 to 1 to have the game kept going here at home." But many players believed that a quick end to the season was inevitable, and they began lining up jobs at steel mills and shipyards.

Barney Dreyfuss, president of the Pittsburgh Pirates, warned of a crisis in baseball:

> It has been pointed out several times by those most strenuously engaged in war affairs, including I understand President Wilson and Secretary of War Baker, that wholesome sports, and diverting entertainments, should be continued for the benefit of the relaxation and recreation they furnish to those who remain at home. It might be, therefore, that if proper steps were taken, it would be considered that ball players were in a degree worthy of consideration in this respect, as their services are unique and unusual, and cannot be performed properly except by one who has a natural ability for the work and has developed it to the limit of his skill.

Some journalists gloated about "the new life facing 'Mr. Baseball Player' . . . [who] must become accustomed to bunking in uppers, eating simple grub, waiting for trains, having his stipend shaved to conform to contingencies, and submitting to hardships." Such star players as Christy Mathewson, Ty Cobb, Grover Cleveland "Pete" Alexander, Eddie Collins, and Denton "Cy" Young volunteered for duty and only heightened the public displeasure with those who stayed behind.

Uncertainty reigned, but the War Department said that a ruling on ballplayers couldn't be made until there was a test case: A player needed to be drafted and then appeal his case to the local draft board. That player was Eddie Ainsmith, a twenty-eight-year-old catcher for the Washington Senators, who had duly registered with District of Columbia Local Board No. 9 on June 5, 1917, and received a 4-A deferment. After the Work-or-Fight Order, Ainsmith appeared before the board along with his manager, Clark Griffith, who said that his catcher and his dependents would experience financial hardships if he were placed in the hands of Uncle

Sam. The board, however, ruled that Ainsmith had to either find war-related employment or be drafted. The Safe Shelter Leagues beckoned. Baseball held its breath, but the flight from the dugouts to the factories continued.

OVER HERE. On the afternoon of July 3, 1917, the Cleveland Indians were edging the St. Louis Browns, 5–4, at Sportsman's Park. Some four miles away, in the community of East St. Louis, white mobs were attacking black residents and destroying their homes. The draft had created a labor shortage in many northern cities, and southern black people were lured to the new employment opportunities. When white workers at several East St. Louis factories went on strike in early 1917, black workers were recruited as replacements. Rumors grew about black men raping white women. The violence crested on July 3 as black people, including women and children, were killed indiscriminately. The rioters cut the hoses of fire trucks and then burned black-owned homes and stores, killing the people who tried to escape the flames. Several men were lynched. Neither the local police nor the National Guard moved to protect the black citizens. The next day, a *St. Louis Post-Dispatch* reporter wrote, "For an hour and a half last evening I saw the massacre of helpless negroes at Broadway and Fourth Street, in downtown East St. Louis, where a black skin was a death warrant." A subsequent congressional investigation could come up with no precise death toll, but the estimates from several sources ranged from forty to two hundred. Some six thousand black people were left homeless.

Wally Pipp, Yankees twenty-five-year-old slugging first baseman, departed for Fore River. Other Yankees, including twenty-five-year-old pitcher Ed Monroe, twenty-two-year-old outfielder Wilson "Chick" Fewster, thirty-year-old outfielder Hugh High, and twenty-five-year-old pitcher Allen Russell, signed on with Sparrows Point. When Dodgers pitcher Al Mamaux, twenty-five, left for Fore River, owner Ebbets was furious and asked the federal government for protection against the hemorrhaging to the industrial leagues. The *Washington Times* said, "It is reported by nearly every Major League manager that in Philadelphia, Boston, and New York alleged agents from Steel League teams fairly swarm around the hotels frequented by the ball players, offering them fat jobs and military compensation." And the *Pittsburgh Press* noted, "The Bethlehem Steel Corporation never does things in halves. Whether it be making steel for Uncle Sam's ships, shrapnel to fire at the Hun, or baseball, Charles Schwab's workers can be counted on to do something big. Now the Bethlehem Steel Baseball League, which is soon to open its second year, is offering salaries almost as big as the major leagues."

On June 3, Red Sox pitching ace Hubert "Dutch" Leonard threw a no-hitter, the second of his career, against the Detroit Tigers. He told sportswriters after the game that he had been inspired to do it in response to criticism from a Boston sportswriter, who had said he was "hopeless because his arm was gone." Leonard, twenty-six, threw shutouts on June 9 and June 13, but on June 30, he left for Fore River, where he became the ace of that pitching staff. His duties at the shipyard were a mystery.

Another late June departure was Jeff Tesreau, the number-two pitcher (behind Mathewson, a future Hall of Famer) on the New York Giants. Tesreau, a burly farm boy with a hard-to-hit spitball, feuded with Giants manager John McGraw and left because he said that he was "disgusted with baseball and wanted to get into some other business"—but he promptly signed on with the Steel League's Bethlehem team. Sportswriters believed that Tesreau was being paid more money than he had received from the Giants. Although he was offered his job back with the Giants in 1919, Tesreau spurned it and decided to coach at Dartmouth College.

A frustrated Ban Johnson appealed directly to Schwab and said that he came away with assurances that neither the BSL nor the DRSL would direct its appeals to Major League players with a 1-A draft status. Johnson added that Schwab had told him that he was unaware of the talent exodus to the shipyards he oversaw. This claim prompted a retort from Comiskey, who charged that Schwab was fully aware of the recruiting efforts: "I know of my own personal knowledge that the matter was brought to their attention." However, by this time, Schwab was overseeing the nation's shipbuilding efforts for President Wilson and had little time for baseball's problems. The BSL was under the control of Eugene Grace, Schwab's successor at Bethlehem Steel, and as a baseball man himself, he was aggressively seeking talent for his baseball league. At least on the surface, Schwab appeared to be only indirectly connected to the DRSL through his job as a shipbuilding czar. But the Major League owners and officials saw his hand in both industrial leagues.

One of the first voices of criticism against the defecting players belonged to Mathewson, the Hall of Fame pitcher who was managing the Cincinnati Reds in 1918; he said that only baseball players above the draft age should be in the steel and shipyard leagues: "If the Government needs these [draft-age players] in the shipbuilding industry it should have them. Even if they are wanted merely to furnish entertainment to the workers, they should go if the Government wants them. But if mere ability to play base ball is going to win exemption for these men, what are the thousands of men in the country, who are not ball players and had no such chance to win exemption, going to think about it?" Mathewson, who was thirty-seven years old, would enlist in the army later that year and go to France.

One of the most important impacts that World War I had on baseball was that it made Ruth an everyday player. Anticipating the loss of key players to the service, Ed Barrow, the Red Sox' new manager, began, with some hesitation, experimenting with playing Ruth in the field on some of the days he was not pitching. When outfielder George "Duffy" Lewis, one of Boston's best hitters, enlisted in the navy, Barrow looked around for a substitute. Right fielder Harry Hooper suggested Ruth as a permanent replacement. Not only was he one of the Major League's best pitchers; he was also showing great prowess as a batter and even greater promise as a power hitter.

In his first three seasons with the Red Sox, Ruth averaged a home run in every thirty-nine plate appearances; his teammates averaged one in every 459 at-bats. So, on May 6, Barrow placed Ruth in the lineup at first base, batting sixth in the order. It was the first time Ruth appeared in a game in a position other than pitcher. Before long, Ruth became an everyday player on the field. His pitching days were over—although not for long. "The war that had rearranged borders and affected so many lives had affected his too. It had put him in the outfield," writes Leigh Montville in *The Big Bam: The Life and Times of Babe Ruth.*

The worldwide pandemic known as the Spanish flu did not significantly affect the United States until the fall of 1918, but it did make an appearance that spring around Boston, which was a busy port for American servicemen returning from Europe. Thanks to Ruth's status as a married man exempting him from the military draft in the opening period of America's entry into the war, Ruth's first brush with the effects of the war came at home and proved just as dangerous. On a warm spring day when there was no ball game, Ruth and his wife went to the beach, and that night, he came down with severe aches and pains and a fever of 104 degrees. It was the Spanish flu. Oliver Barney, the Red

Sox' physician, prescribed a treatment of coating Ruth's throat with a solution containing silver nitrate. Ruth experienced severe pain and was rushed to Massachusetts General Hospital, where he nearly died.

Randy Roberts, a Purdue University history professor and the author of *War Fever: Boston, Baseball, and America in the Shadow of the Great War*, says that the cure was worse than the disease: "Silver nitrate could be effective, but you had to be really careful with it, because if you did it too liberally and it dripped down into a patient's throat, it could kill them. That's what happened to Ruth. It wasn't the flu that almost got him, it was that treatment with silver nitrate." Roberts observes that misinformation was a problem in 1918, just as it was with COVID-19 in the twenty-first century:

> It spread so quickly. People were suddenly wearing masks and there were all kinds of different theories about how to get rid of it. There were all these wives' tales or whatever you want to call them. Some people said, "Get your tonsils removed and you won't get it." Other people said, "Chew tobacco." Some people said, "You have to get your teeth removed." I'm imagining people with no teeth and no tonsils chewing tobacco. I don't know how that would go. But the rumors, the fear, was pretty much the same. That's what you get in a pandemic. There was just a lack of information.

Leonard's departure to Fore River left a void in the Red Sox mound corps, and Barrow asked Ruth to resume pitching as well as playing in the outfield. However, Ruth was enjoying his new role as an everyday player and refused. A standoff ensued, and relations between manager and player became increasingly frosty. When Barrow suggested that Ruth was being selfish and irresponsible, Ruth responded, "I'm tired." Barrow retorted, "If you'd get to bed on time once in a while, you wouldn't be so damned tired."

The turmoil reached crisis level on July 2, when the Red Sox were playing in Washington against the Senators. In the sixth inning, with the Sox losing by three runs, Barrow ordered Ruth to wait out the pitcher, hoping for a walk to start a rally. Instead, Ruth, characteristically, swung at the first pitch; he then proceeded to strike out on the next two. When the slugger returned to the dugout, an infuriated Barrow yelled, "That was a bum play!"

"Don't call me a bum, not unless you want to get a punch in the nose," Ruth shouted.

"That'll cost you $500."

"The hell it will. I quit!"

Ruth walked out of the dugout, dressed in the clubhouse, and watched the last three innings from the stands with a friend. Then, he checked out of the team motel and went to be with his father in Baltimore. When the Red Sox left Washington for a series in Philadelphia, Ruth was not with the team.

For a few days in July, it appeared that Ruth had jumped to the shipyard league.

Still fuming that night from his father's Baltimore bar, Ruth wired Frank Miller, manager of the DRSL's Chester club, asking to join the team. Ruth, like other Major League stars, had already been aggressively courted by agents from both the BSL and the DRSL, and he knew that he could land a job in the shipyard. The next day, the *Chester Times* exclaimed, "Manager Frank Miller, of the Chester Combination received a telegram from 'Babe' Ruth, the home run clouter and twirler of the Boston Americans, that he will come from Washington to play with the Chester team. It is understood that Miller has signed him for the remainder of the season." The news did not sit well with Barrow or owner Frazee, who had come to Philadelphia. When a reporter asked Frazee about Ruth's walkout, he responded, "Where is this shipyard? Who's in charge of the team? I've got a contract with Ruth and they have no right to use him." Frazee warned that he would seek a court injunction preventing his star from playing for Chester, and if Ruth did take the field on July 4, Frazee would sue the shipyard.

Reporters caught up with Ruth in Baltimore as he was tending his father's bar and asked him whether he was trying to evade the draft. "No, that's not it at all," he replied. "I've been deferred because I'm married, but we've all signed up anyway to do our bit after the season is over. Anytime they want me, all they'll have to do is call me and I'll go." That night, Heinie Wagner, Red Sox shortstop and a good friend of Ruth, was sent to Baltimore by Barrow on a recruiting trip. Wagner quickly persuaded Ruth to return to the Red Sox, and the pair took a train to Philadelphia, arriving around 2:00 A.M. But Barrow was still indignant and resentful, and he refused to put Ruth in the lineup for either of the doubleheader games with the Athletics on July 4. Ruth's motives for flirting with the shipyard team are unclear, but for the rest of the season, Ruth pitched and played in the outfield when he wasn't on the mound, as Barrow had demanded.

Despite Ruth's quick turnaround, there was broad speculation that he was making a move to avoid the draft—especially since it came the day after the Work-or-Fight Order took effect on July 1. Many Americans were angered that Ruth and other baseball stars, including Joe Jackson and Rogers Hornsby, were not heeding the call to arms. Grantland Rice, the legendary sportswriter who was now in the army and serving as the sports editor of *Stars and Stripes,* said that many soldiers were "bitter against star ball players, fighters, and motion picture actors who had remained behind." The armed forces newspapers editorialized, "Sport as a spectacle, sport as an entertainment for the sideliners, has passed on and out. Its glamour in a competitive way has faded." Then, *Stars and Stripes* dropped the sports page entirely, saying that there was no room in its newspaper for draft-age men who were playing baseball while others were "charging machine guns and plugging along through shrapnel or grinding out 12-hour details 200 miles in the rear."

In early July, the National Commission—a flawed, little-heeded MLB committee that would be abolished two years later—told all sixteen teams to have their players submit affidavits to their local draft boards, requesting draft-exempt status. The boilerplate affidavits suggested that drafting any Major League ballplayer "w[ould] cause substantial financial loss not only to himself and to his employer but to the general prosperity of the country" and that "affiant further says that he is not skilled in any employment other than the one in which he is now engaged."

But a few days later, Secretary of War Newton Baker rejected the National Commission's contentions, ruling that playing baseball was not an essential occupation and that "ball players are men of unusual physical ability, dexterity, and alertness, just the type needed to help in the game of war at home or abroad." Although the ruling in the Ainsmith test case was not entirely unexpected, MLB was nevertheless stunned. "Baseball Will Lose Its Brightest Stars," headlined the *Boston Post*. "Practically every baseball player of note in both major leagues is affected by Secretary Baker's interpretation of the work or fight order—Cobb, Speaker, Collins, Ruth, Hooper, Baker, Mays, Scott, Johnson, Sisler—there is no need to continue the list. All must quit baseball."

Baseball had wanted it both ways: that baseball be considered an essential American training opportunity for battle-ready men and a welcome respite from deadly world events. But it could not be both, and Uncle Sam was making the choice and choosing the former. So, baseball's first instinct was to take away the latter.

American League President Ban Johnson, without consulting the magnates, declared that all eight teams would suspend operations within three days. James Dunn, owner of the Cleveland Indians, agreed, but others fought back. Red Sox owner Frazee declared, "No one has the right to take the dictatorial stand that the A.L. will close its ball parks at such and such date." The baseball brass sought some sort of extension, even two weeks, that would allow them to make a more orderly transition. Frazee headed a group that appealed to Crowder, head of the draft machinery, asking whether the season would be extended until October 15. They defended "the national pastime" as "second in its hold upon the masses only to the theatres . . . [supported by the] patronage of millions of American citizens whose fanatical devotion to the game has become proverbial." A compromise was reached that permitted baseball to run its regular season until Labor Day, September 2, and then have a World Series, starting September 5. The magnates were delighted. It was a green light to cash out and come up with a plan for the following season. Each team would play thirty fewer games, but the turnstiles would be active for another six weeks.

The players knew that they would come under the Work-or-Fight Order in a few weeks. Hugh S. Fullerton wrote in the *Boston American*: "On or before September 3 we must bid farewell to the present generation of baseball stars. Unless the war ends suddenly, this generation of athletes will never be seen again." The war, of course, did end in November. But no one in July knew that would be the case.

A popular song appeared:

A player of the major leagues was packing up his grip,
And making preparations for a weary ocean trip;
An edict had been issued that he'd have to fight or toil,
To help his Uncle Sam-u-el defend his native soil.
He wasn't used to working, so, he said he'd rather scrap;
In fact, he would enjoy it, being quite a husky chap.

So he was not downhearted as he packed his clothes away,
And as he bid his friends farewell
He chirped this roundelay:

Oh, for years I've been in clover,
But I'll soon be going over;
I have heard the call of duty
I'll soon be on my way.

But believe me when I say it,
I will learn the game and play it,
And for all my tribulations
Kaiser Bill will have to pay.

He has knocked my bankroll silly,
And I have it in for Willy
So I've laid aside the spangles
For a khaki suit of dun;
Kaiser Bill I'm not afraid of
And I'll show the stuff I'm made of,
For I've put away the willow
For a bayonet and gun.

OVER HERE. In August 1917, some 450 sharecroppers and tenant farmers, most of them illiterate or barely literate, were arrested in Oklahoma and imprisoned for taking part in an anti-draft protest that came to be called the Green Corn Rebellion. Some received prison terms of up to ten years.

With the Ainsmith ruling, the persuasive recruiting agents from the steel mills and shipyards had even more powerful ammunition, and the exodus of Major Leaguers to the essential industries and their baseball fields escalated. Walter Holke, Giants first baseman, was ordered before his draft board and instructed to either seek essential employment or receive a 1-A classification. He took a job at the Bethlehem Steel Mill and also played ball. Holke's experience prompted other Major Leaguers to move on to the steel mills and shipyards before their draft boards could designate them as 1-A.

Hornsby, who had just turned twenty-two, was playing shortstop for the Cardinals in July. Branch Rickey, Cardinals president, had just turned down an offer from the Chicago Cubs to pay $50,000 for the services of the only Cardinal star who seemed draft-proof. Since January, Hornsby had been sheltered from military service with a Class 3 deferment, and he had been able to reject the entreaties of the industrial league recruiters. He had told the draft board that he was the sole financial support for his mother, whom he described as "crippled," and his sister. The *Pittsburgh Press* noted, "Rog is very devoted to his mother and every night is found next to her bed reading her books." Hornsby also claimed that his $7,500 annual baseball salary enabled him to buy Liberty bonds and otherwise donate money to the war effort. But then, just as playing baseball was being declared not essential, Hornsby's draft board in Fort Worth, Texas, informed him that he had been reclassified as 1-A and should either get a war-essential job or be drafted into the military. Rickey's biographer Lee Lowenfish says that Hornsby was "the first Major League player to be told bluntly by the authorities, 'Work or Fight.'" Hornsby said that he would finish the season with the Cardinals, as he was allowed, and then seek employment with the Harlan Shipyard in Wilmington.

It was, indeed, a whole new ball game.

4

THE TEAMS

By 1900, baseball was hugely popular throughout the United States. Our national pastime was just that. "It's our game, America's game," declared Walt Whitman. "It belongs as much to our institutions, fits into them as significantly, as our Constitution's law; is just as important in the sum total of our historic life." Baseball's pervasiveness cannot be exaggerated. Teams and leagues existed at all levels of society—high schools, colleges, prisons, churches, and, especially, businesses and industries, where players punched clocks in steel mills, coal mines, shipyards, and factories.

"Every section of the country saw good industrial baseball," says writer Jim Leeke. "The Northeast and Atlantic Seaboard had three leagues, the Northwest and West Coast a total of four, the Great Lakes two, and the Gulf Coast one. A pair of small leagues scattered across remote Southwestern mining towns plus one league in the Midwest brought the total to thirteen circuits, comprising seventy-four teams altogether." In a 1914 amateur championship game in Cleveland, some eighty-three thousand fans showed up to watch Telling's Strollers defeat Hanna's Street Cleaners.

Well-attended games on hardscrabble diamonds offered recreation for workers, entertainment for townsfolk, and publicity for the companies. Success on the field translated into company morale and community pride.

Baseball historian Heather S. Shores says that there are two differing opinions on the rise of company baseball:

> Many support the idea that company management created baseball teams in order to promote teamwork, to keep workers away from labor unions, and to teach immigrant workers how to be "real Americans." In addition, these scholars argue that organized sports such as baseball helped workers fresh from the fields become more dependent on and accustomed to mill and village life as opposed to the often nomadic, seasonal schedule of the agrarian worker. These historians believe that mills organized baseball teams "in an effort to transform sandlot games into a sport sponsored by and identified with the company." The same authors contend that baseball kept workers from being "idle" outside of business hours, encouraged them to stay at the mill for longer periods of employment, and, according to one manager from a South Carolina mill in 1910, taught employees from rural areas the "rules" of mill life.
>
> Other scholars argue that mill baseball was not an advantage for the company alone. They believe mill baseball was more worker-oriented than some people have realized, at least for the players. Many mill baseball managers and players in South Carolina had the bargaining power to secure good financial support for the team each season. In Dalton, Georgia, players seemed to have more control over their situation in the mill, using their talents on the field to alter the "rules" of their lives off the field. For example, the best players enjoyed some opportunities for mobility within

the mill network as different companies sought to recruit them from competitors.

There were also two distinct models for industrial baseball. In one, the players actually had jobs they performed; in the other, they played baseball—period.

The textile mills region of the southeastern United States became a company baseball hotbed. Joe Jackson got his start in the game by playing for the Brandon Textile Mill in West Greenville, South Carolina. The fathers of two of baseball's greatest players, Willie Mays and Mickey Mantle, played for company teams. Elvin "Mutt" Mantle worked in a zinc mine in Commerce, Oklahoma, and William Howard "Cat" Mays worked in a steel mill and played center field in the industrial leagues around Birmingham, Alabama. As Allen Barra points out in his 2014 book, *Mickey and Willie: Mantle and Mays, the Parallel Lives of Baseball's Golden Age*, the two superstars "were both the products of two generations of ball-playing men, and both honed their skills through competition with industrial leagues. Though neither of them was a member of an industrial league team, their fathers, uncles, and close friends played industrial ball, and Mickey and Willie played with and against them. Mantle and Mays were probably the last products of the great age of industrial league baseball that died out a few years after World War II."

Industrial baseball faded due to unionization, mechanization, increased mobility from the automobile, and the rise of other sports, especially football. Interestingly, industrial baseball continues to flourish in Japan under the umbrella of the Japan Amateur Baseball Association. The teams are company-owned, and their players are paid as company workers, not as baseball players.

But during World War I, Pennsylvania, and especially the greater Philadelphia area, was fertile ground for industrial baseball. The eight-team Northeast Manufacturers League was organized in 1917 and provided draft-proof jobs for young men. Its teams were

Fayette R. Plumb (cast steel tools maker), Frankford Arsenal (ammunition), Schwarz Wheel (auto and truck wheels), Quaker City (rubber company), E. H. Fitler (cordage works), Abrasive Company (grinding wheels manufacturer), Frankford Laundry, and Super Glass (auto safety glass).

But no industrial league, before or since, ever approached the substance of the Bethlehem Steel League (BSL) of 1918. It is widely considered to be the best independent baseball circuit of all time. Each of the six teams' rosters was heavily populated by Major Leaguers and talented minor league players. The games attracted crowds of between two thousand and three thousand fans, and occasionally the attendance was much larger, especially as the pennant races tightened and individual games became more important. Playing fields were either refurbished or built anew to accommodate the onlookers. There was a twenty-game regular season schedule that ran through late August.

At each plant, top executives were placed in positions to supervise and improve their teams.

BETHLEHEM. Eugene Grace, the acting Bethlehem Steel CEO, brought in Tom Keady, the baseball coach at nearby Lehigh University, to assemble the Bethlehem mill team. He was aided by Billy Sheridan, who managed other employee sports teams at the corporation.

The pitching staff was anchored by Jeff Tesreau (age thirty in 1918), the New York Giants right-hander who left his team in June after feuding with manager John McGraw. Fred Anderson (age thirty-two), another Giants pitcher, was a spitball artist. He was also a dentist, and he would leave the Bethlehem team in mid-season to join the Army Dental Corps. Stan Baumgartner (age twenty-three), who had pitched for the Phillies in 1916, was a left-hander who had developed his pitching arm as a boy on a paper route by throwing the newspapers up flights of stairs. He would leave baseball and became a sportswriter for the *Philadelphia Inquirer.*

One of Bethlehem Steel's minor league pitchers was Al Schacht (age twenty-five), who would play briefly with the Washington Senators in 1919 and then go on to a comedy career as the "Clown Prince of Baseball." Schacht came to Bethlehem believing that he was draft-exempt because of a hearing deficiency. But he was drafted into the army in July and spent the duration of the war in the United States, playing baseball on military teams.

The team's first baseman was Walter Holke (age twenty-five), a switch-hitter who left the New York Giants and went to Bethlehem after being ordered before his draft board and told to enlist in the army or seek essential employment. Two years later, Holke would set the Major League Baseball (MLB) record for most putouts by an infielder (forty-six) in the course of a twenty-six-inning game between the Dodgers and the Braves. At second base for Bethlehem was Paddy Baumann (age thirty-two), who had just closed out his big league career with the Yankees. Monroe Randolph "Dolly" Stark (age thirty-three), who had played for the Cleveland Indians and the Dodgers between 1909 and 1912, was at shortstop. He would go on to become a Major League umpire. Earl Blackburn (age twenty-six), who played for the Cubs in 1917, was the team's catcher.

The outfielders were George Twombly (age twenty-six), who had played for the Reds, the Braves, and the Senators; Ed Fitzpatrick (age twenty-eight), Braves right fielder; and Cy Seymour (age forty-six), a left-handed hitter who played in the majors between 1896 and 1913 for the Giants, the Reds, and the Braves. He had a lifetime batting average of .303.

Keady also recruited several of the players on his Lehigh University team to play for Bethlehem. One of them was Sam Fishburn (age twenty-five), a shortstop who would go on to play for the St. Louis Cardinals in 1919.

FORE RIVER. Bethlehem Steel had purchased the Fore River Shipyard in 1913. The general manager of the Fore River team was Joseph P. Kennedy, an assistant manager at the mill and the father of a future U.S. president, John Fitzgerald Kennedy, who had just celebrated his first birthday. Kennedy, who was twenty-nine years old, had lettered in baseball at Harvard while studying economics. When the United States entered the war in 1917, he looked around for a job that would keep him out of the army. He enlisted the support of his father-in-law, John F. Fitzgerald (aka "Honey Fitz"), who was a powerful Democratic politician. Fitzgerald persuaded Charles Schwab to hire his son-in-law as an assistant general manager at an annual salary of $15,000—the equivalent of almost $300,000 in today's purchasing power—even though he had no experience in the shipbuilding industry. Kennedy was so ineffective as a manager that he was placed in charge of the baseball team.

A biographer, Ted Schwarz, puts it this way: "Joe Kennedy did not want to die. He did not want to wear the uniform of his nation. He did not want to test his bravery. . . . He just wanted to make enough money to be a millionaire by the time he was thirty-five."

A strong pitching rotation was headed by Dutch Leonard (age twenty-six), the former Red Sox right-hander who had just pitched a no-hitter against the Detroit Tigers in June, and Al Mamaux (age twenty-five), the Dodgers ace whose departure for Fore River had incensed Charles Ebbets. To lure Leonard, Kennedy offered him $200 a week from the plant and $50 a week from his own pocket. Kennedy believed that "with the addition of this man, it would make the pennant sure." In fact, Fore River finished the year in last place. Leonard pitched for Fore River all summer until he lost his draft exemption, when an investigation by his draft board concluded that he had joined the shipyard team "for no other reason than to 'duck the draft.'"

The Fore River first baseman was Wally Pipp (age twenty-five), a top player with the Yankees who led the American League in home runs in 1916, with twelve, and in 1917, with nine. Before leaving for the shipyard in 1918, Pipp had two home runs and a .304 batting average. Pipp is best known for asking Yankees manager Miller Huggins for a day off in 1925 and being replaced—permanently—by Lou Gehrig. Often at second base for Fore River was Clyde Engle (age twenty-seven), who had retired from the Cleveland Indians after eight Major League seasons. Engle was already famous when, as a member of the Red Sox in the final game of the 1912 World Series, he pinch-hit and lofted a routine fly ball that the Giants outfielder Fred Snodgrass misplayed, and the error led to a Boston victory. It came to be known as the "$30,000 muff"—roughly the difference in the payouts to the winners and losers of the World Series. Larry Kopf (age twenty-seven), a former Cincinnati Reds shortstop, shared that position on Fore River with John Dowd (age twenty-seven), who briefly played shortstop for the Yankees. Ken Nash (age thirty), was a utility infielder who had played at Cleveland alongside Nap Lajoie, the future Hall of Famer. In 1918, Nash played for Fore River while serving as a district judge in Quincy not far from the shipyard. One of the catchers was Tom Daly (age fifty-two), who had a seventeen-year Major League career with the White Sox and the Reds and a lifetime batting average of .278.

Olaf Henriksen (age thirty), a Red Sox outfielder, was a contact hitter with speed on the bases. He, too, was remembered for the last game of the 1912 World Series, for singling in the tying run against Giants great Christy Mathewson. He is the only Major League player born in Denmark. Another Fore River outfielder was Merwin Jacobson (age twenty-four), a good left-handed hitter who played for the Giants and the Cubs in 1918 before heading to Fore River. Also leaving Major League teams in 1918 to patrol the outfield for Fore River were the Dodgers' Jim Hickman (age twenty-six) and the Braves' Joe Connolly (age twenty-five). Lee King (age twenty-five), who had played with the Pirates, the Giants, and the Phillies, was another Fore River outfielder.

LEBANON. On paper, defending champion Lebanon was one of the strongest teams in the league, employing many major and minor league talents. This was due in no small part to the efforts of Charles Schaeffer "Pop" Kelchner, a teetotaling college professor who spoke seven languages and went on to become the most successful scout in Major League history. In a scouting career that began in 1912 and ran until 1958, Kelchner signed eighty-six prospects who made it to Major League teams. His finds included four Hall of Fame members—Chief Bender, Walter "Rabbit" Maranville, Stan Musial, and Lewis "Hack" Wilson. Bethlehem Steel had purchased the Lebanon, Pennsylvania, plant in 1917.

Lebanon's primary strength was pitching. Hank Ritter (age twenty-five in 1918), a right-hander who played for the Giants in 1916, had a 4–1 lifetime record. Jess Buckles (age twenty-eight) was a lefty who appeared in two games for the Yankees in 1916. Alex Main (age thirty-three) left the Phillies on June 29 to come to Lebanon. The right-hander never returned to the Major Leagues. Righty Dick Rudolph (age thirty), who had pinpoint control and led the Braves to a pennant and World Series victory in 1914, left Boston for Lebanon in mid-July. Norm Plitt (age twenty-five), a rookie right-hander, pitched one game for the Dodgers before heading to Lebanon in June. Plitt had been signed by Kelchner.

First base was occupied by Tom Jones (age forty-four), who had eight Major League seasons with the Browns and the Tigers. He was one of the best defensive first basemen in the game. Derrill "Del" Pratt, one of the best second basemen in baseball, played for the Yankees for three months before taking off for the steel mill. Mike Mowrey (age thirty-four) was a clutch hitter and considered one of the game's best third basemen; he was especially skilled at defending against bunts—a vital responsibility in the Dead Ball Era (roughly the first fifteen years of the twentieth century, when the baseballs were less lively by design and by overuse). Another infielder, Ambrose McConnell (age thirty-five), was five feet five and known as "Midget." He had played for the White Sox. Ed Miller (age thirty) left the Cleveland Indians on July 3 to come to Lebanon. He lived in nearby Annville, Pennsylvania. Another Lebanon infielder was Ed Lennox (age thirty-four), who was a good hitter and had played for the Athletics and the Cubs.

Lebanon secured a rotation of three active Major Leaguers behind the plate. Steve O'Neill (age twenty-six), who had gone to work in a coal mine at the age of ten before turning to baseball, established a reputation for a strong arm and intelligent signal-calling with the Indians. Much later, as a manager, he would lead the 1945 Detroit Tigers to victory in the World Series. Another catcher was George "Ducky" Hale (age twenty-three), who left the Browns for Pennsylvania on June 26. Sam Agnew (age thirty-one), Babe Ruth's Red Sox batterymate, joined Lebanon in September after their Red Sox won the World Series.

In a Major League career that ran from 1912 to 1925, outfielder Joe Schultz (age twenty-five) played for seven National League teams—all except the Giants. His namesake son would become a catcher for the Pirates. Also in the outfield for Lebanon was Earl Potteiger, a minor leaguer, who would go on to play in the National Football League (NFL) and then coach the NFL's New York Giants to their first championship in 1927. Right field was usually occupied by Charlie Babington (age thirty-three), who had played with the Giants in 1915.

Babe Ruth (age twenty-four) and Rogers Hornsby (age twenty-two) would play for Lebanon in the 1918 postseason.

SPARROWS POINT. Bethlehem Steel acquired Sparrows Point Shipyard in Maryland in 1916 as part of its purchase of Maryland Steel. Sparrows Point relied less on Major League talent than did its competitors. According to *Maryland Historical Magazine*, "Sparrows Point management, unlike some of its opposition, seemed pleased that they had 'not gone in for big raids' on major league clubs." Nevertheless, Sparrows Point did make a big dent in the Yankees roster.

One of the first to jump was Ed Monroe (age twenty-three), a right-handed pitcher who left the Yankees on May 17. George Mogridge (age twenty-nine) was a Yankees pitcher whom Ruth called the best left-hander in the American League. Like Ruth, he was also a good hitter. Clarence "Lefty" Russell (age twenty-eight) so impressed Athletics manager Connie Mack in 1910 that he paid $12,000 for Russell's contract, the most ever spent for a player up to that point. Lefty's brother, Allen Russell (age twenty-five), was a spitball specialist with the Yankees who would go on to become one of baseball's first relief specialists. All joined Sparrows Point for the 1918 season.

Chick Fewster (age twenty-two) was a Yankees second baseman, whose claim to fame would come when he became the first batter to step into the box at Yankee Stadium when it opened in 1923. Also in the infield was Jimmy "Runt" Walsh (age thirty-two), who had played for the Phillies and the Cardinals and was one of only about a dozen players ever to appear in all nine positions in a single season. Walsh was also an accomplished sign-stealer. Aleck Smith (age forty-seven), who had played nine Major League seasons with six teams, did most of the catching. He would die of a heart attack in 1919.

As a Detroit Tigers outfielder, Hugh High (age twenty-nine) sometimes substituted for Ty Cobb when the Georgia Peach was injured or holding out for more money. High was traded to the

Yankees, but when they tried to trade him to the lowly Athletics in 1918, he jumped to Sparrows Point. Two of High's brothers, Andy and Charlie, also were Major Leaguers. Johnny Priest (age twenty-seven), a Yankees infielder, was moved to the outfield at Sparrows Point.

STEELTON. The mill was a colossal presence in Steelton, Pennsylvania, a tiny borough of two square miles on the Susquehanna River, near Harrisburg. George Cockhill, a former National League umpire, managed Steelton with help from player-manager Steve Yerkes (age thirty), who last played for the Cubs in 1916. The Steelton roster was replete with former, active, and future Major Leaguers.

The pitching rotation was headed by two left-handers, Eddie Plank (age forty-two), a future Hall of Famer, and George Pierce (age thirty), who had played for the Cubs and the Cardinals before retiring in 1917. Also on the mound for Steelton was Jack Knight (age twenty-three), a right-hander with the Phillies.

Yerkes was the first player to get a hit when Fenway Park opened in 1912. He had just turned down an offer from Branch Rickey to play for the Cardinals and moved to his hometown of Reading, Pennsylvania, to join Steelton. His BSL season would end abruptly when he injured his leg in July and had to be carried off the field. Another Steelton infielder was Joe McCarthy (age thirty-one), who had been playing for the Louisville Colonels of the American Association. McCarthy never made it to the big league as a player, but he would go on to a Hall of Fame career managing the great Yankees teams of the 1930s. The shortstop was Wilbur Charles "Roxey" Roach (age thirty-five), who had played for the Senators and thirteen minor league teams.

The Steelton outfield included Harry "Bud" Weiser (age twenty-seven), who broke in with the Phillies in 1915, and Johnny

Beall (age thirty-six), who left the Cardinals for Pennsylvania on July 16. Beall hit the first home run in Chicago's Wrigley Field, in 1914.

Steelton's most versatile player was Herb Hunter (age twenty-two), who could play all positions except pitcher and catcher. He appeared in games for the Giants, the Cardinals, the Red Sox, and the Cubs. Later in life, Hunter became very involved in the movement to bring baseball to Japan.

WILMINGTON. Bethlehem Steel's Harlan plant in Wilmington, Delaware, fielded teams in both industrial baseball leagues: The BSL unit was called Wilmington, and the Delaware River Shipbuilding League (DRSL) entry was known as Harlan. Sometimes, players were maneuvered between the teams for competitive advantage. Wilmington was managed by Fred Payne, who had a Major League playing career with the White Sox and the Tigers and had managed at Syracuse in the New York State League. Payne also took the field for his Wilmington team occasionally, in addition to performing his managerial duties. Wilmington's marquee player was Jackson (age thirty-one), who played more games in the BSL than in the DRSL.

The team's pitching ace was Claude "Lefty" Williams (age twenty-five), who jumped his contract with the Chicago White Sox a few days after he came to Wilmington. A few days earlier, Williams had been a major part of what is considered one of baseball's greatest games. On May 15, 1918, Williams and Mathewson of the Giants engaged in a pitching duel that saw each go eighteen innings before the Giants won on a wild pitch by Williams. Williams would become infamous in 1919, when he lost three games in the World Series and, like Jackson, was banned from baseball forever as part of the Black Sox scandal.

Another good Wilmington pitcher was George Dumont (age twenty-three), a right-hander who was a teammate of Walter

Johnson on the Senators. Joe Lake (age thirty-seven), also right-handed, spent six seasons in MLB, all with losing teams. Rounding out the mound staff was Bob Steele (age twenty-four), a rookie left-hander who left the Giants to come to play in the shipyard.

Lee Dressen (age twenty-nine), a left-handed leadoff hitter and excellent base stealer, was the Tigers' starting first baseman when he opted for Wilmington. Another speedy runner was Gus Getz (age twenty-nine), who could play all infield positions. The shortstop was Jack Martin (age thirty-one), a great fielder and light hitter who played with the Yankees, the Braves, and the Phillies. Another shortstop was Charles "Heinie" Wagner (age thirty-seven), who left the Red Sox after winning the World Series. Infielder Zinn Beck (age thirty-two) left the Yankees for Wilmington.

Wilmington had strong catchers. Ed Gharrity (age twenty-six) caught Johnson and Dumont at Washington. Before coming to Wilmington, Gharrity had only one hit for the Senators in 1918—a pinch-hit double off Ruth. The other catcher was Byrd Lynn (age twenty-nine), Williams's batterymate at the White Sox and a good friend of Jackson. Wilmington's outfield included Ennis Telfair "Rebel" Oakes (age thirty-five), a former Cardinal and good defender who played shallow center field.

The DRSL attracted far fewer Major League players than did the BSL—perhaps twenty-five or thirty active or recently retired players made the shift to the shipyards. However, the ranks of the eight teams were filled by active minor leaguers and semiprofessionals seeking to avoid the military.

The four best teams were Chester Ship, Harlan, Hog Island, and New York Ship. Chester Ship had Harold "Twink" Twining (age twenty-four), a right-handed pitcher who had played briefly with the Cincinnati Reds, and Jim Eschen (age twenty-seven), an outfielder who had a short career with the Cleveland Indians. Other Major Leaguers on Chester Ship were Forrest Cady (age thirty-two), a bullpen catcher with the Athletics; Charles Preston "Press"

Cruthers (age twenty-eight), Athletics second baseman; and Milt Watson (age twenty-eight), a right-handed pitcher who came over from the Phillies. Also on the roster were three Chinese players from Hawaii. Harlan's roster included Fitzpatrick (age twenty-eight), who had three seasons with the Boston Braves, mostly at second base. In addition to Bender (age thirty-five), Hog Island had Hans Lobert (age twenty-seven), who had thirteen years in the majors as a third baseman with the Pirates, the Reds, the Phillies, the Cubs, and the Giants. He was one of the fastest players in baseball, and while he was with the Giants, he won a hundred-yard dash against Jim Thorpe. Also on Hog Island was Ralph "Pep" Young, a switch-hitting second baseman with the Detroit Tigers. Hog Island's player-manager was outfielder Johnny Castle, who had a brief career with the Phillies. New York Ship had William Edward "Wid" Conroy, a former Yankees third baseman. Traylor had pitcher Elwood Marter "Chick" Holmes (age twenty-two), a right-hander who left Mack's Athletics in the middle of 1918.

Harlan was unique because, as the season wore on, it used more Major Leaguers from the plant's BSL Wilmington team. Among the regulars on the Harlan DRSL squad were two young players from Mack's Philadelphia Athletics—Robert Geary (age twenty-seven), a right-handed pitcher, and Merlin Kopp (age twenty-six), a star left fielder. Also on the Harlan roster was George Winter (age forty), a former Red Sox right-handed pitcher who had played with Plank on the Gettysburg College team.

The other teams—Merchant, Pusey & Jones, Sun Ship, and Traylor Ship—had rosters that included many standout minor league players, but they did not fare well against their stronger rivals.

The DRSL was plagued by player-eligibility issues for the entire season. A league rule that a player had to be on the shipyard payroll for fifteen days was adhered to by Jackson, but it also was ignored by others. The problem would lead to a stunning end to the Shipyard League season.

Grover Cleveland Alexander shortly before he was traded to the Cubs by the Phillies. He was drafted and served with the 342nd Field Artillery, Eighty-Ninth Division, in France, where he damaged his pitching arm; he later suffered from post-traumatic stress disorder. Nevertheless, he resumed his career and won 373 games over a twenty-year career. (*"Grover Cleveland Alexander, Philadelphia NL," Courtesy of the Library of Congress Prints and Photographs Division, Washington, D.C., 20540 USA.*)

Charles Albert "Chief" Bender, a Native American from the Ojibwa tribe, was the ace of Connie Mack's Athletics pitching staff before the war. He pitched for the Hog Island shipyard, where it was widely reported that he put in long hours in addition to playing baseball. (*"Chief Bender, Philadelphia AL [baseball]," Courtesy of the Library of Congress Prints and Photographs Division, Washington, D.C., 20540 USA.*)

Left: White Sox owner Charles Comiskey spent lavishly to build a winning team in 1918, only to see it decimated by defections to the Steel and Shipyard Leagues. (*"Charles Comiskey, owner, Chicago AL [baseball]," Courtesy of the Library of Congress Prints and Photographs Division, Washington, D.C., 20540 USA.*)

Right: Major General Enoch Herbert Crowder was the judge advocate general of the U.S. Army from 1911 to 1923 and oversaw the administration of the Selective Service Act of 1917. (*"Crowder, Enoch. General," Courtesy of the Library of Congress Prints and Photographs Division, Washington, D.C., 20540 USA.*)

Lee Dressen was a left-handed first baseman who played for the Cardinals and the Tigers in a five-year Major League career; he joined the Harlan shipyard on June 1, 1918, and never returned to the majors. (*"Lee Dressen, St. Louis NL [baseball] 39," Courtesy of the Library of Congress Prints and Photographs Division, Washington, D.C., 20540 USA.*)

Red Sox owner Harry Frazee threatened to sue the Chester Shipyard team if his star player, George Herman "Babe" Ruth, took the field for the Pennsylvania team. (*"Harry Frazee, Boston AL Team Owner [baseball]," Bain News Service, 1916. Courtesy of the Library of Congress Prints and Photographs Division, Washington, D.C., 20540 USA.*)

Above: Eddie Grant was a Harvard graduate and an outstanding defensive third baseman. After retiring from baseball in 1915, he practiced law in Boston until April 1917, when he enlisted in the army. Grant was killed in the Meuse-Argonne Offensive on October 5, 1918. (*"Eddie Grant, New York NL [baseball]," Courtesy of the Library of Congress Prints and Photographs Division, Washington, D.C., 20540 USA.*)

Left: Hugh High was a good left-handed hitting outfielder. When the Yankees tried to trade him to the lowly Athletics, he went to work at Sparrow Point instead. He never returned to the Major Leagues. (*"Hugh High, New York AL [baseball]," Courtesy of the Library of Congress Prints and Photographs Division, Washington, D.C., 20540 USA.*)

Rogers Hornsby was a twenty-two-year-old superstar who finished the regular National League season with the Cardinals before joining a steel mill team in Reading, Pennsylvania. (*Courtesy of the Queens Borough Public Library, Archives, William V. Cahill Collection.*)

Shoeless Joe Jackson's career batting average of .356 is the fourth highest in Major League history, but he is often remembered for his role in the infamous Black Sox Scandal of 1919. (*"Joe Jackson," Courtesy of the Library of Congress Prints and Photographs Division, Washington, D.C., 20540 USA.*)

Ban Johnson, the founder and first president of the American League, harshly criticized players who jumped to the Steel and Shipyard Leagues. (*"Ban Johnson," Courtesy of the Library of Congress Prints and Photographs Division, Washington, D.C., 20540 USA.*)

Left-hander Herbert "Dutch" Leonard left the Red Sox for the Fore River Shipyard in June 1918; the Red Sox sold his rights to the Tigers before the 1919 season began. (*"Dutch Leonard, Boston AL [baseball]," Courtesy of the Library of Congress Prints and Photographs Division, Washington, D.C., 20540 USA.*)

Byrd Lynn angered White Sox owner Charlie Comiskey when he left the team to join Joe Jackson at the Harlan shipyard. (*"Byrd Lynn, Chicago AL [baseball]," Courtesy of the Library of Congress Prints and Photographs Division, Washington, D.C., 20540 USA.*)

Immortal pitcher Christy Mathewson was managing the Reds when he volunteered for army duty; he was seriously injured in a training accident involving mustard gas. (*"Christy Mathewson, Cincinnati NL [baseball]," Courtesy of the Library of Congress Prints and Photographs Division, Washington, D.C., 20540 USA.*)

Left: Yankees first baseman Wally Pipp was leading the American League in home runs with nine when he left for Fore River Shipbuilding Company of the Bethlehem Steel League. (*"Wally Pipp, New York AL [baseball]," Courtesy of the Library of Congress Prints and Photographs Division, Washington, D.C., 20540 USA.*)

Below: Eddie Plank joined Steelton and became the first Major Leaguer to sign up with the Steel League. He had just retired from a 326-win career that would land him in the Hall of Fame. (*"Eddie Plank, Philadelphia AL [baseball]," Courtesy of the Library of Congress Prints and Photographs Division, Washington, D.C., 20540 USA.*)

Right: Branch Rickey, who would volunteer for the army's Chemical Warfare Unit in 1918, was managing the St. Louis Browns in 1913. (*"Branch Rickey, St. Louis AL [baseball]," Courtesy of the Library of Congress Prints and Photographs Division, Washington, D.C., 20540 USA.*)

Below: In 1918, George Herman "Babe" Ruth was converting from an outstanding pitcher to a great hitter. (*"Babe Ruth," Courtesy of the Library of Congress Prints and Photographs Division, Washington, D.C., 20540 USA.*)

Left: Charles Schwab ordered subordinates at Bethlehem Steel to establish a baseball league and not "bother [him] about details of expense." (*"Charles M. Schwab, 1862–1939," Courtesy of the Library of Congress Prints and Photographs Division, Washington, D.C., 20540 USA.*)

Below: Pitcher Jeff Tesreau left the Giants in May 1918 to play for the Bethlehem team in the Steel League. (*"Charles M. 'Jeff' Tesreau, New York NL [baseball]," Courtesy of the Library of Congress Prints and Photographs Division, Washington, D.C., 20540 USA.*)

Steve Yerkes, recently retired from the Chicago Cubs, was a player-manager for Steelton's entry in the Bethlehem Steel League. (*"Steve Yerkes, Boston AL [baseball]," Courtesy of the Library of Congress Prints and Photographs Division, Washington, D.C., 20540 USA.*)

Before the Yankees play the Red Sox on Opening Day, 1917, Army General Leonard Wood shakes hands with an unidentified Yankees player as Yankees manager Bill Donovan looks on. Standing to the far right are Yankees owners Tillinghast L'Hommedieu Huston and Jacob Ruppert. (*"General Leonard Wood & Wild Bill Donovan, manager, New York AL, at Polo Grounds, New York," Courtesy of the Library of Congress Prints and Photographs Division, Washington, D.C., 20540 USA.*)

Led by an Army drillmaster and a military band, the New York Yankees march onto the Polo Grounds field; it was Opening Day, April 11, 1917. (*"Opening Day Polo Grounds," Courtesy of the Library of Congress Prints and Photographs Division, Washington, D.C., 20540 USA.*)

Pretending their bats are rifles, the Yankees execute dismount drills under the directions of Army Sergeant Smith Gibson. (*"Sgt. Gibson drilling Yankees, 1917," Courtesy of the Library of Congress Prints and Photographs Division, Washington, D.C., 20540 USA.*)

The Yankees drill under the directions of Army Sergeant Smith Gibson. (*"Yankees [drilling], 4/11/17," Courtesy of the Library of Congress Prints and Photographs Division, Washington, D.C., 20540 USA.*)

The Lebanon team in the Bethlehem Steel League was filled with big leaguers, including, briefly, George Herman "Babe" Ruth, third from left in the top row. (*"Some Team," Courtesy of the Lebanon County Historical Society.*)

Saturday Base Ball Game

LEBANON (Bethlehem Steel)

vs.

JIM NASIUM'S BIG LEAGUERS.

Saturday Afternoon, Sept. 27, at Third and Cumberland Sts., Starting at 2:30 O'clock.

Visiting line-up will include such big leaguers as Daubert, 1b.; Doolan, ss.; Knabe, 2b.; Pearce, 3b.; Oldring, lf.; Muench, cf.; Jamieson, rf.; McAvoy, c., and Watson, p.

"Babe" Ruth will be in the line-up for Lebanon.

Help the Lebanon Boys by turning out in large numbers. HEAR THE PATRIOTIC BAND CONCERT.

On September 26, the *Lebanon Daily News* carried an ad for the big game. Babe Ruth suited up for Lebanon in the Bethlehem Steel League. (*Courtesy of the Library of Congress Prints and Photographs Division, Washington, D.C., 20540 USA.*)

Ty Cobb (*left*) poses with Joe Jackson before Cobb and the Tigers square off against Jackson and the White Sox. (*"Ty Cobb, Detroit, and Joe Jackson, Cleveland, standing alongside each other, each holding bats," Courtesy of the Library of Congress Prints and Photographs Division, Washington, D.C., 20540 USA.*)

5

THE SEASON

Despite widespread scorn, especially in newspapers, for the "slackers" in the "Safe Shelter Leagues," the star power in the Bethlehem Steel League (BSL)—and, to a lesser degree, in the Delaware River Shipbuilding League (DRSL)—helped the games find eager audiences. Most Steel League contests drew between three thousand and five thousand spectators. One game in July between Bethlehem and Fore River drew some eighteen thousand fans in Lehigh Stadium. That same afternoon, a few miles away at Philadelphia's Shibe Park, only seven thousand fans showed up to watch the Athletics battle Babe Ruth and the Boston Red Sox.

The Steel League saw numerous disputes over umpiring. Most of the time, the arbiters were local figures and not up to Major League standards. At one game in Wilmington, police had to be called in to protect the umpire from physical harm. But the biggest controversy came over player eligibility, an issue that would alter the seasons of both leagues in dramatic fashions.

Indeed, the Steel League's season began with an eligibility protest.

The game in question—Lebanon versus Wilmington, at Wilmington—was won by the home team, 4–2. Pitcher George Dumont, who had a 1–1 record with the Washington Senators before leaving for the shipyard, scattered nine hits for the victory. The winners scored all their runs in a fourth-inning rally started by Ed Gharrity, who was Dumont's batterymate in Washington but played first base for Wilmington.

The problem was that Dumont and Gharrity had only recently arrived at the shipyard. Indeed, Lebanon manager William G. Maurer claimed that he saw Gharrity arriving on the field just before the game while still carrying his suitcase. Maurer filed a protest with the league, claiming that Dumont and Gharrity had violated the league rule that players had to be on the shipyard payroll fifteen days before being eligible to take the field. The Steel League executive committee upheld the protest and ordered that the game be replayed. Wilmington won the rematch.

Ironically, one spectator at this game was Wilmington's Shoeless Joe Jackson, who was heeding the fifteen-day rule. The *Wilmington Evening News* noted, "The Right Honorable Joseph Jackson hunkered on the bench, wearing shoes and a wistful look as well as civilian's duds. It didn't require an expert to diagnose the reason for the wistful look—Joseph wanted to be in the game, which he will when the legal time comes."

Each of the first three games of the League's season drew about 2,500 fans.

The following week, in the Shipyard League, Jackson once again watched as Harlan defeated Hog Island, 6–4. Despite Jackson's ineligibility, the game was advertised as a meeting between him and Chief Bender. One publicity blurb read, "Fellow fans, lend me your ears; just how does this sound? Joe Jackson holding the ash and Chief Bender shooting the pill." The buildup was enough to attract some five thousand fans. Bender inquired after Jackson, and the two shook hands before the game.

During that weekend, players in the safe shelter leagues received a chilling reminder of the dangers of military enlistment through the tragic story of a fellow ballplayer. News spread that Ralph Sharman, an outfielder for the Philadelphia Athletics, had been killed in a training accident at Camp Sheridan, Alabama. Sharman had made his Major League debut in September 1917 and showed great promise. In thirteen games with the A's, he batted .297 with eleven hits, two doubles, a triple, two runs batted in (RBIs), a stolen base, and three walks. Sharman enlisted in the army after the 1917 season and began artillery training on November 5.

OVER HERE. On the morning of March 4, 1918, Albert Gitchell, an army cook at Camp Funston, Kansas, showed up at the infirmary, complaining of a sore throat, high fever, and headache. By noon, more than a hundred soldiers had joined him there with similar complaints. Gitchell is considered the first case of the Spanish flu in the United States. It is estimated that 675,000 Americans died in the epidemic, part of a worldwide death toll of about five hundred million people.

OVER THERE. Although the origin of the term is uncertain, newspapers began calling American soldiers in France "doughboys," and the term soon caught on with the public. General John J. Pershing had rejected a suggestion that they be called "Sammies." The equivalent for British soldiers was "Tommies," and men from Australia and New Zealand were "diggers."

In 1918, the last Monday in May was designated as Decoration Day to honor the Civil War dead. It would be renamed Memorial

Day in 1971 to honor all men and women who died serving in the U.S. military. The Steel League's holiday schedule was topped by Jackson at last playing his first game for Wilmington. He went hitless, including a first-inning strikeout, and played first base rather than the outfield. It was only appropriate that the newly minted steelworker should shake off some rust. The *Philadelphia Inquirer* reported, "Joe Jackson played his first game as a war worker, but was unable to accomplish anything sensational with the willow, contrary to expectations, as Steelton's outfielders played deep and were able to gather in his vicious long drives." The *Wilmington Morning News* said that one of Jackson's hits would have been a home run, but it was kept in play by a stiff breeze.

Despite widespread scorn for the notion of some big leaguers dodging military service while their teammates fought, the league's star power helped it find an eager audience. The next morning, the *Wilmington Morning News* gushed, "Major League baseball, better than it is out under the big top, was offered up to 5,000 or more wild and wooly fans that crowded into every nook and corner of the Harlan Field yesterday afternoon when Harlan forced Steelton to take the short end of a 2–1 score in a Bethlehem Steel League game."

Jackson would not remain hitless for long. In Week 4, as the Steel League entered into June, Wilmington moved into first place by defeating Sparrows Point, 5–1. Jackson had two hits and would go on to become the undisputed star of the BSL, although at one point he complained, "It's harder to hit in this league than in the American League." He would finish his seventeen-game season with a league-leading batting average of .393.

The Shipyard League received less attention than did the Steel League, but when Harlan beat New York Ship, 4–3, that week, the *Philadelphia Inquirer* took the time to dub it a "slow and lifeless game."

Wilmington consolidated its first-place lead in the standings in Week 5 with a convincing 4–0 win over Lebanon behind Dumont's five-hitter. Bill Ritter was the losing pitcher. Jackson had two hits. Some three thousand fans witnessed the action at Lebanon's Cottage Hill Field. Wilmington boasted a first-place 5–1 record. Meanwhile, Harlan defeated Merchants, 5–1.

OVER THERE. The first major engagement of American troops was the Battle of Belleau Wood, which began on June 6, 1918. The previous month, the German forces had penetrated to within forty-five miles of Paris, and the French were retreating. American Marines and soldiers counterattacked and over the next three weeks drove Germany out of the forested area. The surge marked the end of the stalemate; the tide of the war had turned. At the battle's close, some ten thousand Americans were killed, wounded, or missing in action.

There were many heroes. One of them was Hugh Miller, who had played first base briefly for the Phillies and then spent several seasons in the minor leagues. He enlisted in the Marine Corps in June 1917 and was in the trenches the following March. John B. Sheridan, a sportswriter from Miller's hometown of St. Louis, described his actions at Belleau Wood: "He dashed for the machine-gun positions. His company went after him. The men who were with him say that he performed prodigies of valor, tore right into a machine-gun crew, bayoneted two Huns and took two more prisoners, made them carry their gear and march back to the rear."

For his actions under fire, Miller was awarded the Distinguished Service Cross. The citation read, "Hugh S. Miller, private, Company K, 6th Regiment, United States Marine Corps. In the Bois de Belleau, France, on June 6, 1918, he captured two of the enemy single-handedly. Although ordered to the rear twice because of illness, he returned to his command voluntarily and continued to fight with it vigorously throughout the advance." The medal was pinned on his chest by General Pershing himself. He also received the Navy Cross when it was authorized in 1919.

On a Wednesday in mid-June, Lebanon's Steel League team played an exhibition game against the Brooklyn Royal Giants, a top-ranked professional Negro League team based in New York City. It would be the first of several midweek games between the Giants and the Steel League and the Shipyard League squads.

The Brooklyn Royal Giants were formed in 1905 by John Wilson Connor, the owner of the Brooklyn Royal Café. Initially, the team was chartered not as a moneymaker but as a promotion for the café. Then, in 1914, Connor sold the team to Nat Strong, a white businessman who converted it into a barnstorming club, meaning that it traveled in several eastern states, playing white and black semiprofessional teams. The Giants had no home field, but it became one of the best independent teams in the Negro Leagues and won Eastern League championships in 1914 and 1916.

The Giants, like most Negro League teams, rode to games in junker vehicles because trains were too expensive. Often, the players were not welcome in hotels and restaurants, forcing them to take their meals and sleep in the cars, or they would sleep on the field, using their gloves as pillows. Most of them were playing for the love of the game; remuneration would only cover dinner.

An important part of the Negro barnstorming teams was clowning, and several Giants doubled as comedians who would swing the bat from their knees or with one hand or run the bases clockwise. There was, however, an unwritten rule that baseball professionalism came first and that the comedy could start only when the game was secure.

In one sense, the war was a boon for the Negro Leagues (sometimes called "Blackball") because the sudden need for manpower at northern defense plants drew black migrants from the South, which, in turn, created a larger Negro League fan base with money to buy baseball tickets. But, on the other hand, many of the black players volunteered for military service or were drafted.

Giants player-manager was John Henry Lloyd, who was widely considered the greatest shortstop in Negro Leagues history. No Major Leaguer other than Honus Wagner could match his ability, and one source quoted Wagner as saying that he was honored to be compared to Lloyd. Sometime in the summer of 1918, Lloyd left the Giants to work for the Army Quartermaster Depot in Chicago. He was inducted into the National Baseball Hall of Fame in 1977.

One Giants standout was Richard "Cannonball Dick" Redding, who was regarded as perhaps the fastest pitcher in the history of black baseball. But while his team played exhibitions against the Steel League, Redding was in the army in France. A Giant who did play that summer was another Hall of Famer, catcher Louis Santop, who was Redding's batterymate before the pitcher left for France. Santop could throw a ball from home plate over the center-field fence, but he was best known as Blackball's first legitimate home-run slugger. His towering drives earned him the nickname "Big Bertha," so called after Germany's huge artillery weapon. Santop also was called the "Black Babe Ruth" before Josh Gibson won the same nickname in the 1930s. Santop was inducted into the Hall of Fame in 2006. Another fearsome Giants pitcher was right-hander Frank Wickware, who was also in the army that summer.

Other standout Giants who were on the team that summer included Bill Handy, one of the best second basemen in Blackball; Frank Earle in center field; and Johnny Pugh in right field. Whether they played in the June 13 Lebanon game is uncertain because the *Lebanon Daily News* did not carry a story about the game—even though it had run an advertisement for the game the day before.

The failure to cover this matchup may owe to the reluctance of the time to acknowledge black achievement on an equal playing field with white subjects. Case in point: A few blocks away from the field, Lebanon's Academy of Music had just completed a return engagement of the silent film *The Birth of a Nation*, today notorious for its racist portrayal of black people. Many consider the film's popularity to be one reason for the rebirth of the Ku Klux Klan (KKK). The film became a potent fundraiser for the KKK. Performances were at 2:15 P.M. and 8:15 P.M.; the price of admission ranged from fifteen cents for the gallery to fifty cents for the main floor. In its *Daily News* advertisement, the theater stipulated, "No more than 10 seats sold to one person." President Woodrow Wilson was an admirer of the film.

OVER HERE. At the outset of the war, black leaders urged young men to enlist and to seek to unite with white soldiers in the hope that the joint patriotic venture might help race relations. But the military remained rigorously segregated, which discouraged black volunteers. Black soldiers were initially denied participation in combat and restricted to menial tasks, such as working as mess boys. Under intense pressure from the National Association for the Advancement of Colored People (NAACP), President Wilson opened a single training camp for black officers. Two black divisions were raised, but they were not allowed to train together, so black soldiers remained a minority at every post.

OVER THERE. Thousands of American soldiers died of Spanish flu on troop ships bound for France in 1918. "What the men aboard these death ships experienced can scarcely be imagined," writes historian G. J. Meyer. "Men crammed together in impossibly tight quarters would turn dark blue, a sign of cyanosis, the failure of the lungs to supply oxygen to the blood and more often than not fatal. Men would go wild with delirium, bleed from their noses, then ears, and even their eyes. . . . Men would be buried at sea in an uninterrupted stream." The army refused to take precautions, arguing that cutting the flow of troops would be a morale boost for Germany and that every man who died at sea "just as surely played his part as his comrades who died in France."

Wilmington got a major boost in mid-June when pitcher Lefty Williams and his batterymate Byrd Lynn infuriated Charles Comiskey by leaving the White Sox for jobs in its shipyard. But in the team's 4–2 victory over Fore River, Jackson stole the show, literally. He singled and then stole second base, third base, and home, moving one sports scribe to comment in the *Wilmington Evening Journal* that Jackson "would have probably stole [*sic*] Murphy's chest protector, leg guard and mask if they had been of any use to him." Jackson, an accomplished base runner, would lead the league in stolen bases with eight. After the game, a concert by the Harlan band was followed by a minstrel show. Lest anyone read Lebanon's exhibition against the barnstorming Giants as a sign that the Steel League was immune to the culture of the time, minstrel shows featured entertainers in blackface who sang, danced, and performed comedy routines employing stereotypical versions of black Americans.

At the end of the day, Wilmington remained in first place, with a 5–1 record, followed by Lebanon, 4–3; Steelton, 3–3; Bethlehem, 3–4; Fore River, 2–4; and Sparrows Point, 2–4.

As could be said for any of his Wilmington teammates in the Steel League, Jackson could have played for Harlan's Shipyard League entry, but so far, he had not. The *Philadelphia Public Ledger* opined, "Manager [Fred] Gallagher, of Harlan-Bethlehem, of the Ship League, will find it necessary to requisition the services of Joe Jackson if the Wilmington aggregation is to stay in the running at all."

The following weekend, Week 7, Bethlehem edged Wilmington 1–0 behind the pitching of Jeff Tesreau, who had just left the New York Giants. Dumont shut out Bethlehem for eight innings, but second baseman Ed Fitzpatrick (Braves) led off the ninth with a single, moved to second on a sacrifice by Paddy Baumann (Yankees), and scored the winning run on a single by Dave Wright, the catcher. Jackson had one of the seven hits off Tesreau. The game had to be stopped three times because of steady rain. Nevertheless, some 1,800 fans watched the entire game at Bethlehem.

The competitiveness shown by Steel League team managers extended to other agents of their respective teams. As the July 1 date for the Work-or-Fight Order loomed, the Steel League teams hired professional scouts and managers to intensify their efforts to recruit Major Leaguers. Yankees business manager Harry Sparrow received an anonymous tip to be on the lookout "for a man in a gray suit and soft hat, who will try to interview the Yankee players between games. He is a shipyard agent, and his name is Petty." The *New York Sun* reported, "Divers [*sic*] stars have been asked to name their terms and the agents do not take one 'nay' as final. We know of a player who was approached three times in as many days. He got rid of the pest by threatening bodily harm. A pitcher for one of the New York clubs has been asked to fill out his contract to work for a shipbuilding team." The *Washington Times* offered this insight: "It is reported by nearly every major league manager that in Philadelphia, Boston, and New York, alleged agents from Steel League teams fairly swarm around the hotels frequented by the ball players, offering them fat jobs and military compensation."

In the spring of 1918, Ruth became a hero. He forsook the pitcher's mound for the batter's box, and—with his sweeping, powerful, flawless swing—re-created the national pastime in his image. Gone was the time-honored strategy of bunts and tiny hits to move the runners along. In its place was the colossus of a Ruthian clout over the fence. Ruth literally rewrote the dimensions of the game, and he would become the greatest hero in the history of American sports—and a genuine American legend.

Ruth always got good press. According to Georgia Tech history professor Johnny Smith, "The sports writers, particularly in Boston, constructed an image of him as all that is good in America. His power at the plate at a time when no one else was hitting home runs or swinging for the fences the way that he did becomes a metaphor for American manpower in the war. The difference in the war is going to be American manhood, American strength. Ruth demonstrates that the powerful American man is what decides the outcome on the ball field just like powerful American manhood will decide the outcome in this war."

Journalists made direct connections between Ruth's prowess at home plate and the doughboys fighting in France. "The story of Babe Ruth's mighty hitting, his Homeric smashes, kindles a glow in the hearts of all those who know baseball," rhapsodized the *Boston Herald and Journal.* "In Italy, in Normandy, in Alsace, and in a hundred camps along the firing line, men meet and ask for the latest news of the gifted hitter of home runs. The story of each succeeding circuit clout is received with acclaim. It lightens and breaks the dangerous tension of a soldier's duty and it's not stretching a point to say that in his own inimitable way, the Colossus is contributing a worthwhile gift to the morale of Uncle Sam's fighting men both in the new and the old world. He is the hero of all present-day baseball."

OVER HERE. Germany and all things German became evil in the eyes of the American people, thanks to relentless government propaganda. Scores of communities changed their names to throw off names deemed too Teutonic. Berlin, Iowa, became Lincoln, while Berlin, Michigan, became Marne; Germantown, California, became Artois; Breslau, New York, became Lindenhurst; and Bismarck, Pennsylvania, became Quentin.

Even players changed their names. Heinie Zimmerman and Heinie Groh became Henrys. Churches dropped German-language services, and public schools stopped teaching German. Sauerkraut was renamed "liberty cabbage," and dachshunds were called "liberty hounds." Academics enamored by Johann Wolfgang von Goethe, Rainer Maria Rilke, or Johann Christoph Friedrich von Schiller had their patriotism challenged. Works by George Frideric Handel, Ludwig van Beethoven, Johann Strauss, and Robert Schumann were *verboten* in concert halls.

Baseball climbed on the bandwagon. *Baseball Magazine* ran anti-German songs and crude cartoons and said that if Germany only played baseball, "it might have saved her the stain of mangled Belgium and of the *Lusitania*." Leon Cadore, a pitcher with the Brooklyn Dodgers, opined, "The American Army is a thinking army, composed of men who are intelligent and have the proper spirit. In Germany, everything is one vast scheme of iron discipline." The *Boston Transcript* tortured a metaphor when it commented, "Germany is trying to steal home by spiking the catcher. And she can't understand why the bleachers are jeering at her."

The nation's editorialists were only too glad to join the anti-German chorus. Editorials like this one in the *Providence Journal* popped up everywhere: "We are at war with the most merciless and inhuman nation in the world. Hundreds of thousands of its people in this country want to see America humiliated and beaten to her knees, and they are doing and will do, everything in their power to bring this about. Take nothing for granted. Energy and alertness in this direction may save the life of your son, your husband or your brother."

The barbs were aimed at some two-and-a-half million Americans who were born in Germany, their six million children, and millions more with less direct German backgrounds.

Anti-German passions were fueled by Allied propaganda, which reached absurd levels. One claim was that German soldiers had replaced church bells in Belgium with hanging nuns. Another was that Germany had a "corpse factory," where German soldiers killed in action were dispatched so their bodies could be converted into explosives, boot polish, and other war materials. In the long run, these preposterous tales backfired, according to historian Daniel Wrinn: "After the war, people realized that much of the news concerning the war, and the German enemy had been outright lies. Newspapers would never be so openly trusted again. This attitude persisted into the early stages of the second world war. This meant that when the stories of German death camps first broke, they were widely disbelieved."

Upholding his heroic status, the sports scribes played down Ruth's German background, never calling him by his birth name, George Herman. "During the last two years of the war, when any Teutonic-sounding name provoked suspicions of disloyalty, and the phrase 'German-American' became a pejorative, 'the Babe' served him well," says Randy Roberts, a Purdue University history professor and the author of *War Fever: Boston, Baseball, and America in the Shadow of the Great War.* "It Americanized his last name and advertised his nonthreatening personality. Privately, he spoke German on occasion among friends or at his father's Baltimore saloon, but he never said anything publicly about his ancestors. Besides, he was not German-American. He was the Babe."

War correspondents said that the question they most often got from the troops was about the Babe. "Every night at eleven, a wireless report went out from Arlington to navy ships at sea," according to Roberts. "It included a final score summary of the day's contests. Just the game scores—except for Boston. For the Red Sox, the wireless operator included whether or not Babe had clouted another home run. In an odd twist of fate and wartime circumstances, the wayward kid from Baltimore, the son of a German-American saloonkeeper, had become a hero even to sailors and soldiers fighting to make the world safe for democracy."

Despite his continued eligibility, Jackson had never played in a regular-season game for Harlan's Shipyard League team—for one main reason. Many of the Harlan games were played on Sundays, and he had other plans for that day. During his time in Wilmington, Jackson often left town on weekends at his own expense to play in exhibition games and raise money for the Red Cross and other war-related charities. He was a regular Sunday fixture that summer on the roster of the Reading Steel Casting team, where he drew crowds as large as fourteen thousand. A company executive said that his presence was an important morale booster for the mills and factories in the Reading Area. He noted that the men were working seventy hours a week, with Sunday as their only day off. With nothing to entertain them, they took to heavy drinking, and as a result, factories had high absentee rates on Mondays. After Jackson began playing at Reading, absenteeism dropped, and production rose at the plants. At the end of the season, the vice president of Reading Steel Casting wrote a letter to Harlan Shipbuilding, thanking the company for allowing Jackson to play there and describing how beneficial it had been to workers' morale. Jackson received a copy of this letter. "Joe could have used the letter to offset his critics, but he never did," notes Donald Gropman in his biography *Say It Ain't So, Joe!*

In Shipyard League action, Chester Ship won its seventh straight game, handing Harlan a 3–0 loss with Twink Twining (ex-Reds) tossing a five-hitter before a crowd of five thousand. Chester scored all its runs in the third inning, when Harlan's Williams (White Sox) suffered control problems, walking two and hitting another. Twining also managed two hits in his own at-bats.

In the days before the Chester-Harlan matchup, the *Philadelphia Public Ledger* speculated that the game would attract "the largest crowd that ever witnessed a game in Wilmington" and that it was "almost a certainty that Joe Jackson and other big leaguers w[ould] appear." "I don't care who they play," snapped Chester manager Frank Miller. "We are going to win." Harlan manager Fred Gallagher said that if his club lost, he would "quit the league."

At game time, Jackson's close friend from the White Sox, catcher Lynn, was in the Harlan lineup, but Jackson was not because he was with the Steel League's Wilmington team in Bethlehem. Despite the loss, Harlan did stay in the league—wisely, as it turned out.

OVER HERE. Historian Frederick Lewis Allen notes that the average working man at this time was in, one sense, a prisoner:

> For when a man built a mill or factory, around which there grew up a mill village or factory town, those who came to work for him were in great degree imprisoned by their choice. They did not own the tools with which they worked, and therefore were dependent on what employment the mill offered; and anyhow there was not enough work in such a community for all who would be looking for it if the mill shut down. And if their wages were really low they could not af-

ford to look elsewhere for a job. So they ceased to be free agents. They were at their employer's mercy. The code of conduct for the day did not require him to feel any responsibility for what happened to them.

On Week 7, the last weekend in June, Sparrows Point bested Wilmington, 7–5, in what the *Wilmington Evening Journal* described as "one of the best games of the season in the Steel League," adding that "the infield work of both teams was sensational." Sparrows Point turned three double plays. Leading the Sparrows Point offense were three New York Yankees—John Priest, Chick Fewster, and Hugh High. Jackson had three hits, including a double, but in the fifth inning, he was ruled out for leaving the base path. As the July 1 deadline for the Work-or-Fight Order drew close, the exodus of American and National League players to the Steel League accelerated. The *Evening Journal* noted that the lineups of Sparrows Point and Wilmington consisted mostly of active and former Major Leaguers, which "pleased the 4000 fans."

Wilmington was now 5–3 and tied for first in the BSL. Harlan was also 5–3, but sitting in fourth place in the Shipyard League.

Steelton defeated Wilmington twice in a Week 8 doubleheader to drop Jackson's team to third place. Jackson had two hits on the day.

When the second half of the season opened on July 7, Jackson mustered a single and two walks to help Wilmington overcome first-place Lebanon, 9–4, and tighten the race for the Steel League pennant. Wilmington battered Alex Main (Phillies) and Jess Buckles (ex-Yankees) for nine hits, including a home run, three triples, and two doubles. Although on the roster as a pitcher, Joe Lake (ex-Tigers) made two sparkling defensive plays as a catcher for the winners.

That same day, Harlan reached a low point in the season by losing 2–0 to previously winless Pusey & Jones. Harlan had only three hits, two of them by Lynn (White Sox). P&J fans threw a raucous celebration in the shipyard following the game.

During the ensuing week, Jackson and Williams journeyed to Boston, where the White Sox were playing the Red Sox. The *Washington Times* reported:

> Joe Jackson and Lefty Williams, young shipbuilders, are in Boston, and visited with the White Sox, but failed to pay their respects to manager Rowland and did not call at Fenway Park. Jackson and Williams explained that they are members of a crew aboard a ship that was engaged in its trial trip and that their coming had nothing to do with the national game. The former White Sox contented themselves with gossiping with the fellows on the veranda of the hotel. Both were tanned, looked in excellent health and physical condition, and both expressed their satisfaction in the work in which they are now engaged.

OVER THERE. Johnny Overton, a national champion track star at Yale University, who set the world records for the indoor mile run and indoor thousand-yard run in 1917, was killed on July 19 during the Second Battle of the Marne. Overton, a Marine lieutenant, was hit by a shell fragment near his heart. He was awarded the Navy Cross, the Distinguished Service Cross, and the Croix de Guerre with Palm from the French Army. He was twenty-four years old.

The umpiring once came into question in Week 10 at Wilmington, where the home team won 2–1 over Bethlehem. Dumont pitched a two-hitter and drove in the winning run with a controversial triple. A record crowd of 4,500 was on hand, and those who could not find seats encircled the field, sitting on the grass.

The crowd was not roped off from the playing field. This circumstance, according to the *Allentown Democrat*, was "responsible for near-riots on several occasions." The paper said that the work of the umpires, particularly the plate umpire, "was erratic and almost resulted in calling the game off." With Wilmington leading 1–0 in the third inning, Bethlehem third baseman Baumann (ex-Yankees) singled and scored on a triple to deep center field by second baseman Fitzpatrick (Braves). But the umpire ruled that the ball rolled into the crowd, limited Fitzpatrick to a double, and ordered Baumann back to third. The inning ended without Bethlehem scoring. Bethlehem filed a protest, but it was denied. In the seventh inning, with the score tied 1–1, Dumont apparently drove in the winning run with a triple to deep center field, but the umpire initially ruled that the ball went into the crowd and Dumont was limited to a ground-rule double—as Fitzpatrick had been in the third inning. However, at this point, Jackson raced onto the field, pointed to a spot on it, and said that was where the ball had landed. The umpire agreed and ordered Dumont to third base and the runner home with the go-ahead run. Several Bethlehem players threatened the umpire physically, and he had to be protected by two policemen. The next day's *Wilmington News* praised Jackson's "quick thinking and great knowledge of the game." Catcher Joe Lake (ex-Tigers) had two hits for the winners. Tesreau took the loss for Wilmington.

Standings: Steelton, 9–5; Wilmington, 7–6; Bethlehem, 7–7; Lebanon, 5–6; Sparrows Point, 6–8; Fore River, 5–7.

In Shipyard League play, Harlan made a significant change that would be expanded in the weeks to come; three players from the Wilmington Steel League team were moved over to play for the Harlan Shipyard League nine, which went on to beat Pusey & Jones, 5–2, with Williams (White Sox) pitching a five-hitter. George Mangus (ex-Phillies) had two hits for Harlan, and Lynn

(White Sox) was Williams's batterymate. Some 3,500 spectators showed up for this match.

Harlan was still in fourth place, at 6–5.

In mid-July, the Shipyard League's Eligibility Committee dropped a bombshell, figuratively speaking, ruling on the use of ineligible players. Chester was ordered to forfeit a game to Hog Island, Merchant to forfeit a game to New York Ship, and Sun Ship to forfeit a game to Harlan. It had been caution over eligibility that had kept Jackson from taking the field at the start of the season, and now that decision seemed prudent indeed. Moreover, the league withheld a decision until a later date regarding two Chester victories over Harlan. Harlan, only two games out of first place, smelled blood. One of its last three games was against a formidable opponent, New York Ship, but the other two were against two weaker teams, Sun Ship and the winless Traylor.

Harlan easily defeated Sun Ship, 9–0. Williams (White Sox) pitched the two-hit shutout and was opposed on the mound by a Sun Ship pitcher who played for the Swarthmore College team. Williams also had a double and a home run. Once again, three Steel League players suited up to play for Harlan. The following week, Traylor was unable to play, having just lost five players to the army. Two thousand Harlan fans were dismissed from the stands after waiting an hour for the game to begin. The victories and committee rulings brought Harlan's record to 9–4, behind Chester, New York Ship, and Hog Island.

There was a fascinating twist to a Chester–Hog Island game on August 4. Scott Perry, a right-handed pitcher who was on the roster of the last-place Philadelphia Athletics, pitched in relief for Chester. He gave up a three-run triple immediately and did not distinguish himself for the rest of the game. As a minor leaguer in 1917, Perry had supplemented his income for his growing family by bouncing around industrial league teams, and he apparently continued this practice as a Major Leaguer in 1918. Nevertheless, Perry managed to win twenty games for the hapless A's.

All summer long, Perry was the central figure in a dispute over his ownership between the A's and the Boston Braves. The case was not settled until October, but notably it led to the creation of a commissioner to oversee both Major Leagues. As *Baseball Magazine* put it, "Why, in the name of all that is sensible, couldn't the two contending clubs have reached the same amicable settlement in June, not in October? Two second-division, sub-cellar clubs of jassaks and little monkeys, fighting over a solitary pitcher, and temporarily wrecking the whole fabric of baseball by their obstinacy! Aw, what's the use? Yes, baseball DOES need a housecleaning—needs somebody in charge who can choke off . . . crass and blithering idiocy, and do it with an iron hand!"

Throughout the summer and fall, Perry would face batters in the Steel and Shipyard Leagues. One of them would be Ruth.

OVER THERE. "I found a *New York Herald* paper, which must've arrived before the war. I read and re-read it several times. The baseball scores drew my attention for hours. The blow-by-blow story of Zimmerman of the Cubs getting benched for arguing with the umpire was just as interesting as if it'd happened yesterday." —diary of an American soldier

---

On Sunday, August 4, the Harlan Shipyard management in Wilmington decided to test Delaware's Sunday blue laws, which banned worldly activity, such as baseball, on the Sabbath. The two Harlan teams—Wilmington Shipyard in the Steel League and Harlan Shipyard in the Shipbuilder's League—played each other in an exhibition game that was won by the Steel League nine, 5–4. The game was intended to raise funds for a program that provided cigarettes to servicemen. After the game, some $300 was turned over to the Soldier's Smoke Fund. Before the game began, local police took down the names of the players and umpires breaking the state's blue law. They were all arrested and spent the night in jail before being released. Jackson was in Pennsylvania, playing for the Reading Steel Casting team. The next day, the *Wilmington Morning News* reported, "Three thousand fans and a squad of city police saw Wilmington's first Sunday ball game. After nine innings and $315 for the Smoke Fund, twenty-one players willingly underwent arrest and spent a night in jail. They were released the next day. Also arrested were the umpire and John L. Collyer, head of Safety, Welfare and Employment at the plant."

The religious opponents of Sunday baseball claimed that it defamed the Sabbath. Historians Peter T. Dalleo and J. Vincent Watchorn III note that arguments in favor of Sunday baseball took several paths.

The most common argument offered by supporters of Sunday baseball revolved around the rationale that players, workers, and fans could reduce wartime tensions by attending sports events. Wilmington's Chamber of Commerce and the War Shipping Committee openly claimed that "Sunday baseball is essential to create a spirit of enthusiasm among the shipbuilders." Plant managers offered yet another perspective: Sunday games, they argued, cut down on absenteeism and kept employees away from saloons and drinking. Sober men were more efficient Monday morning workers. Other proponents of Sunday ball placed the issue in the context of class conflicts. Colonel George Elliott, director of the Wilmington Young Men's Christian Association (YMCA), speaking to the anti-democratic nature of the blue laws, argued, "The fact that rich men played golf and tennis while the poor man was deprived of playing baseball or witnessing a game established a class system that is to be regretted . . . and ought to be avoided."

The blue laws were upheld by the courts, and while they were often not enforced, they stayed on the books in Delaware until 1941. The legislature passed a bill repealing the laws after the state attorney ordered a crackdown that resulted in the owner of a gas station being arrested by police right after he had fueled their squad cars at his gas station.

OVER THERE. For the men of the American Expeditionary Forces, baseball was a means of boosting morale. The military created seventy-seven baseball diamonds in France, and on any given day, two hundred or more games were played there. John Cutchins, an infantry officer, reported a spirited game between two teams of Americans near the Alsace front. Guarding against an enemy attack, the ball players carried their gas masks over their shoulders. At one point, a patrolling German plane swooped down for a look.

The "slacker" issue did not leave baseball in the summer of 1918, even after the Work-or-Fight Order went into effect. Headlines complained of "Players Camouflaged as Shipbuilders." On August 5, the *Harrisburg Evening News* ran an editorial on the sports page next to write-ups of the Steel League games. Noting that the Steel League was sometimes called the "Bomb Proof League" because its players were perceived as slackers, it suggested, "It is quite likely that there will be a better feeling all around if the Government insists on a little more work and a little less baseball out of the men who have sought out the jobs which will keep them safely on this side of the Atlantic."

As far away as Utah, an *Ogden Standard* sportswriter said, "I cannot see how some of the baseball heroes have got the nerve to appear in public. Some of them have lied to the draft boards and have been convicted of lying. Yet they go on and play ball and resist every effort made to induct them into the service. Some of them have been pilloried all over the country. Yet they go out calmly and play ball in front of good Americans. Great 200-pound trained athletes playing baseball while 18-year-old boys are dying in the trenches!"

The Sporting News carried a satirical poem, which was a takeoff on Felicia Hemans's Victorian poem "Casabianca," about a young ball player who had not joined the army:

Some more bold, fearless athletes of note
Have gone to captivate the kaiser's goat
And save the world from Hun autocracy
By smearing gobs of paint upon a boat. . . .
The boy who stood upon the burning deck,
When all about him was a flaming wreck,
Was out of luck—he could not smite the ball
Nor swing a brush and draw a big league check.

And *The Sporting News* offered this further bit of sarcasm: "Blue stars indicate on a service flag players who have gone into the service, gold stars indicate those who have lost their lives making the fight for civilization. If it were not that saffron might be mistaken for a gold color it would be suggested that 'yaller' stars be imposed on service flags to demonstrate the players that have left the club to work for the 'steal' league."

Beneath the headline "Pershing's Boys Can't See Why Athletes Get Big Salaries, While They Fight for America," *Stars and Stripes* wrote:

> There is no place left for the Cobbs, the Ruths, and the Johnsons in the ease and safety of home when the Ryans, the Smiths, the Larsens, the Bemsteins, and others are charging machine-guns and plugging along through shrapnel or

> grinding out 12-hour details 200 miles in the rear. Back home the sight of a high fly drifting into the late sun may still have its thrill for a few. But over here the all-absorbing factors are shrapnel, high explosives, machine gun bullets, trench digging, stable cleaning, nursing, training back of the lines, and other endless details throughout France from the base ports to beyond the Marne.

Frank Bancroft, business manager of the Cincinnati Reds, had this question for his boss, owner August Herrmann: "Cannot something be done to stop these robbers getting players under pretext of helping win the war? It is a joke and I don't believe the heads at Washington would sanction contract jumping and slacking if it was put to them as it ought to be. The Kaiser may be rotten but doubt if he would harbor a lot of crooks and hate to believe the U.S. Government will."

Several steel mill teams tried to sign Ty Cobb, but he refused them all and told an interviewer in Philadelphia, "I will never join any of these steel plants or shipyards, for such work would keep me in this country, and the line of service which I desire is to be 'over there.'" However, Cobb finished the season with the Detroit Tigers before enlisting in September, and he did not arrive in France until very near the war's end.

Hog Island manager Johnny Castle felt constrained to defend his team:

> We are making no effort to sign star players. We have certain rules to follow and we live up to them. No preference is shown, no overture is made, and a ball player will have to work just as hard as anyone else in the yard. If any new men wish to enter this work, they can start at about $35 per week, and they will earn every cent they get. If they show

> any unusual ability, they will receive more pay. Not one cent extra will be paid to ballplayers. Hans Lobert, former New York Giant third baseman, and Chief Bender, the great Indian pitcher who performed so well for Connie Mack's team, are on the job from morning until night and play ball on their off days. That's how things are done at Hog Island.

On August 14, Charles Schwab's subordinate, Vice President Howard Conley of the Emergency Fleet Corporation, said that the employment of Major League players in shipyards "more for the purpose of bolstering up their teams than to expedite the shipbuilding program" would no longer be tolerated. He ordered that the ballplayers be placed on the same footing as other workmen and that higher salaries to lure the players not be reimbursed by the corporation.

In Week 13, Wilmington edged Fore River, 7–5, as Jackson drove in the winning runs in the eighth inning with a two-run double. The following week, Wilmington would fall to Bethlehem in a game marred by near riots. Bethlehem's Tesreau held the visitors to four hits, including two by Jackson. Sam Fishburn, the future St. Louis Cardinal, had four hits for Bethlehem. The game was held up in the fourth inning for about five minutes when the Wilmington team disputed the decision of the umpire, calling right fielder Gharrity (Senators) out on strikes. Gharrity's teammate Lake (ex-Tigers) became enraged and struck the umpire in the back of the neck, knocking him to the ground. "This nearly caused a riot," the *Baltimore Sun* reported, "but the field was cleared and the game resumed." The *Allentown Democrat* opined, "The unsportsmanlike conduct of the Wilmington catcher was resented by the crowd and only the promptness of the police prevented a riot."

OVER THERE. The noted World War I poet Wilfred Owen captures the horror of trench warfare in "*Dulce et Decorum est*":

Bent double, like old beggars under sacks,
Knock-kneed, coughing like hags, we cursed through
sludge,
Till on the haunting flares we turned our backs,
And towards our distant rest began to trudge.
Men marched asleep. Many had lost their boots
But limped on, blood-shod.
All went lame; all blind;
Drunk with fatigue; deaf even to the hoots
Of gas-shells dropping softly behind.

Gas! GAS! Quick, boys!—
An ecstasy of fumbling
Fitting the clumsy helmets just in time,
But someone still was yelling out and stumbling
And flound'ring like a man in fire or lime.—
Dim through the misty panes and thick green light,
As under a green sea, I saw him drowning.
In all my dreams before my helpless sight,
He plunges at me, guttering, choking, drowning.
If in some smothering dreams, you too could pace
Behind the wagon that we flung him in,
And watch the white eyes writhing in his face,
His hanging face, like a devil's sick of sin;
If you could hear, at every jolt, the blood
Come gargling from the froth-corrupted lungs,
Obscene as cancer, bitter as the cud
Of vile, incurable sores on innocent tongues,—
My friend, you would not tell with such high zest

To children ardent for some desperate glory,
The old Lie: Dulce et decorum est
Pro patria mori.

Owen was wounded in France and was treated for shell shock. He returned to action and was killed one week before the armistice.

The Shipyard League's Eligibility Committee struck again on August 22, taking two more games away from Chester Ship, dropping them into fourth place with an 8–6 record and putting them out of the running for the championship. The *Chester Times* complained, "There is no denying but Chester was the best team. It is unfortunate that a league of this kind should have elected such an incompetent set of officials who might do well in deciding a game of ceckers [*sic*], but are way off in baseball." The complaint was justified in that the eligibility rules were never clearly defined and only sporadically enforced. The committee also took two games away from Hog Island, ending its chance for the pennant.

When the smoke cleared, New York Ship and Harlan were tied for first place, with 11–3 records. A one-game playoff to decide the DRSL Championship was held at the Strawbridge & Clothier Athletic Field in Philadelphia. The game was a 5–0 blowout because Harlan moved its entire Steel League team, with one exception, but including Jackson, over to play in the Shipyard League Championship. The move prompted *Philadelphia Inquirer* sportswriter Edgar Wolfe to wonder in print: "Just what the eligibility rules of the Shipyard League are we do not know, but Chester must have committed murder if they were found guilty enough to have their games thrown out, while the acts of Harlan in reinforcing its team with players from another league solely for the decisive championship contest can be considered innocent." He likened the mismatch to pitting the Boston Red Sox against a college team.

With a sharp-breaking curve ball, Dumont pitched the shutout. The game was scoreless after three innings, but in the fourth, with a man on third base, Jackson was intentionally walked and then engineered a double steal, which scored Harlan's first run. Jackson then scored on a double by Lynn (White Sox). Gharrity (Senators) homered over the left-field fence in the fifth. Jackson doubled and scored in the sixth. Wilmington scored its final run in the ninth on a wild pitch.

The victory sent Harlan into a best-of-five series for the Atlantic Coast Shipyard Championship.

OVER HERE. The DRSL game was interrupted briefly when Eddie Collins, the Chicago White Sox outfielder, walked into the ballpark in his U.S. Marine uniform. A wave of patriotic cheering erupted as his former teammates, Jackson and Lynn, watched from the field. Collins, a future Hall of Famer, had just enlisted and missed the final eighteen White Sox games.

On the weekend following the DRSL playoff, Harlan's Major Leaguers were back in the Steel League, defeating Sparrows Point, 4–1. Wilmington was led by Jackson, who hit two towering home runs and also added a double. The *Harrisburg Telegraph* said that Jackson's round-trippers were "the longest hits ever made at Wilmington." The *Wilmington News-Journal* said that Jackson's second home run "so enthused the crowd, that they collected a large purse and presented it to the slugger."

The Steel League was to close out its season with the possibility of a three-way tie for first place, as Wilmington prepared to take on Steelton.

However, Steelton put an end to that possibility three days later by climactically defeating Wilmington, 3–2, in eleven innings. Williams pitched well for Wilmington, striking out fourteen batters, but he had trouble with third baseman Jack Knight (ex-Yankees). In the first inning, Jackson crashed into the center field wall while chasing down a triple by Knight. With the score tied 2–2 in the eleventh, Joe McCarthy lifted a fly ball to right field that dropped for a triple when Jackson and Gharrity (Senators) collided. McCarthy raced to third base, and Knight singled him home for the decisive tally. His two collisions clearly weighing on him, Jackson limped off the field as the game ended. The latter collision may have owed to Gharrity playing catcher, not outfielder, over his career with the Senators.

The Steel League Executive Committee decided that the pennant would be decided by a best-of-three playoff between Steelton and Bethlehem, beginning on Saturday, September 7. Steelton won a coin toss and chose to have the first game played at its home field of Cottage Hill. The second game would be at Schwab Field in Bethlehem, and the possible third contest would be at a neutral field; the use of Philadelphia's Shibe Park was under discussion. The gate receipts from the first game would go to the Steelton Red Cross, and those of the second game would be donated to a Bethlehem club that provided services to local enlisted men.

OVER THERE. John Cooper, a catcher who was signed by the White Sox but never made it to the Major Leagues, was killed on September 2 while serving as a private with the Eleventh Infantry Regiment of the Fifth Division in France.

The Major Leagues struggled through the 1918 season, which was shortened by two weeks, suffering from poor attendance and rosters depleted by enlistments, the draft, and flights to the Steel and Shipyard Leagues. The teams repeopled their lineups with players of less ability, less experience, or both. The New York Giants got off to a strong start defending their National League championship. They were in first place, with an 18–1 record, on June 1. But then first baseman Walter Holke and pitchers Jeff Tesreau and Bob Steele jumped to the Steel League, and others, such as John "Rube" Benton and Jesse Barnes, went into the military.

The Chicago Cubs, on the other hand, found themselves in a strong position. They were lightly hit by losses to the military and industrial leagues and had stocked up on pitchers in the off-season. Two of those acquisitions were James "Hippo" Vaughn and George "Lefty" Tyler, who had the two lowest earned run averages in the league and combined for a total of forty-one victories. Right-hander Claude Hendrix added twenty more to that total.

Across town, the White Sox experienced a dramatic drop, losing Jackson, Williams, and Lynn to the Steel League and getting subpar performances from those who remained.

They ended up in sixth place.

Over in the American League, the Red Sox and their new pitcher-outfielder, Ruth, were locked in a tight pennant race with the Cleveland Indians. Ruth the Hitter batted an even .300 and was credited with eleven home runs to lead the league. That total is deceptive, however, because Ruth hit two more home runs. But they came in extra innings, with a man on first base, and under the rules of the day, once the winning run crossed home plate, the game was over, and the de facto home run was scored as a triple. Ruth the Pitcher won thirteen games and had a season earned run average of 2.22.

The regular Major League season ended on September 2, and hundreds of players found themselves subject to the Work-or-Fight Order. Many sought defense-industry jobs to avoid the draft. So concerned were the members of the second-place

Cleveland Indians that they canceled a doubleheader with the St. Louis Browns rather than risk the chance of losing out on the favored jobs. "The Indians preferred to take a chance on losing second place rather than take a chance with the work or fight order," *The Sporting News* smirked. "[Manager Lee] Fohl's workers were more anxious about getting into useful employment than they were worried over the prospect of things coming out that way in baseball."

6

POSTSEASON AND PEACE

As summer was stepping aside to make way for autumn, three championships were decided on baseball diamonds in Boston, Chicago, New York, Philadelphia, Bethlehem, and Steelton. The games were played at a time when the American expeditionary forces were engaged in their heaviest and most important action of the war.

The *Harrisburg Telegraph* proclaimed that the Bethlehem Steel League (BSL) Championship game would be "the greatest game of ball ever played in this vicinity," and then it added, dubiously, "The Bethlehem Steel League officials, from Mr. Schwab on down, were almost as much concerned about the game as in the producing of war materials."

It was the opening game of the best-of-three Steel League Championship: Steelton versus Bethlehem. Four umpires were brought in for the playoffs, including Augie Moran, who had worked in the National League for several years and would be behind the plate.

The first game was in Steelton, the second a week later in Bethlehem, and if a third game were necessary, it would be played in Philadelphia at Shibe Park.

Steelton won the first game, 2–1, in a dramatic pitch-for-pitch struggle between the home team's George Pierce (ex-Cardinals) and Bethlehem's Jeff Tesreau (Giants). Steelton scored both of its runs in the first inning. Second baseman Joe McCarthy and third baseman Jack Knight, a minor leaguer who would go on to play for the Phillies, the Cardinals, and the Braves, each singled, and then left fielder Johnny Beall (Cardinals) was walked to fill the bases. First baseman Dick Kauffman (ex-Browns) singled to right field, scoring McCarthy and Knight. Bethlehem scored its lone run in the second inning on a double by third baseman Paddy Baumann (Yankees), a sacrifice fly by first baseman Walter Holke (Giants), and a fielder's choice groundout. From there, both pitchers shut the door on scoring for the rest of the game. Beall and Kauffman had two hits for the winners. Catcher Earl Blackburn (ex-Cubs) had two hits for Bethlehem and made two standout defensive plays. Bethlehem sent a large contingent of supporters to their rival's home field, filling the grandstand and bleachers. Attendance was estimated at four thousand.

The following Saturday in Bethlehem, Steelton staged a ninth-inning rally, featuring a two-run triple by McCarthy, to win by a score of 5–3 and take the Steel League crown. Bethlehem scored two runs in the fourth inning on two errors, two walks by Pierce, and a base hit by Baumann. Tesreau had not allowed a Steelton base runner until the sixth inning, when Steve Yerkes (ex-Cubs), who had just returned after a mid-season leg injury, hit a single. Steelton tied the game at 3–3 in the eighth inning on a single by Yerkes and a triple by Herb Hunter (Cubs). Eddie Plank, pitching in relief of Pierce, was the winning pitcher and scored the winning run on McCarthy's triple. Attendance at Schwab Field was estimated at six thousand. The game was held up for ten minutes as the opposing managers argued with umpires over ground rules necessitated by overflow crowds in left and center fields.

Eugene Grace, the president of the Bethlehem Steel Corporation, presented each Steelton player with a gold watch.

Harlan brought nine Major Leaguers to the Atlantic Coast Shipyard Championship, most from the Wilmington lineup that had helped Harlan secure their Delaware River Shipbuilding League (DRSL) title. Catcher Joe Lake (ex-Tigers), pitcher George Dumont (Senators), shortstop Zinn Beck (Yankees), first baseman Lee Dressen (Tigers), third baseman Gus Getz (Pirates), right fielder Ed Gharrity (Senators), catcher Byrd Lynn (White Sox), left fielder George Mangus (ex-Phillies), pitcher Lefty Williams (White Sox), and, of course, center fielder Joe Jackson all suited up for the series. Their opponent, Standard Shipbuilding from Staten Island, New York, had three Brooklyn Dodgers on its roster: right fielder Otto Miller, catcher Artie Dede, and pitcher Dan Griner.

Harlan drew first blood in the best-of-five playoff, edging Standard, 3–2, in Philadelphia's Shibe Park, home of the Phillies. Jackson was the opening game's hero, despite his injuries from his final Steel League game. The *Wilmington Evening Journal* carried this lede the next day: "Even as a cripple, Joe Jackson can hit. The former White Sox slugger, with his right foot encased in tape and bandages, went up as a pinch-hitter in the ninth inning on Saturday and made good with a hit." Jackson was credited with a single, but it would have been a double had he been able to run. "It was all he could do to reach first base," the *Philadelphia Inquirer* declared. Jackson was replaced by a pinch runner, who came around to score. Jackson's pinch hit started a Harlan come-from-behind rally. "Harlan looked like a beaten team until Jackson, who is suffering with an injured right foot, took Dumont's place at bat in the ninth," said the *New York Sun*. First baseman Dressen, catcher Lake, and third baseman Getz all had two hits for the winners.

Before the game, six bands participated in a contest to see which could play "Over There" best. The Harlan band won.

The action shifted to the Polo Grounds in New York the next day. Soon after Charles Schwab threw out the first ball, Harlan scored two first-inning runs, and that was enough for a 2–0 victory. Williams spaced five singles over nine innings for the shutout. To open the game, Dressen walked, Getz singled to left field, and Beck singled to right field, scoring Dressen. Getz then raced home on an error by catcher Dede. Jackson rested his injured foot and did not play. The *New York Times* covered the game and reported that "about 2,500 fans, lonesome for baseball since the Giants and Yankees closed up shop, braved the rain and the chill blasts" to watch the action. The massed bands of nine shipyards gave a concert before the game.

Jackson again stole the show in Game 3, leading Harlan to a 4–0 victory and the Atlantic Coast Shipyard Championship.

Jackson hit two home runs over the right-field wall onto Broad Street. His second home run in the eighth inning, which virtually sewed up the game for Harlan, set off a delirious outburst from the home fans. The *Philadelphia Inquirer* gave this description:

> The Harlan rooters went into a frenzy of excitement and virtually showered Joe with greenbacks when he completed his trip around the sacks. Box seat holders on the Harlan side of the field dug deep into their pockets, and before Jackson reached the Harlan bench he was called to the various boxes and had bills of various denominations thrust upon him. Joe was not a bit backward about accepting the financial reward and he made a tour of the boxes collecting everything handed out. After that, he gracefully handed the money over to Mrs. Jackson, who occupied a box. Then beat it for the Harlan dugout. His bit was $60 from enthusiastic Wilmington rooters.

Some 4,500 raucous fans from both sides attended, and many of the Standard rooters brought whistles and horns. In a slap at the hometown Phillies, who had finished their season in sixth place with a losing record, the *Inquirer* said, "There was more honest and sincere rooting in this one contest than there has been at Broad and Huntingdon Streets grounds all season."

Both of Jackson's home runs, plus a double, came off Standard's pitcher Griner, the former Brooklyn Dodger. The *Inquirer* said that the second blast so enraged Griner, "he rushed at Ike Smith of Harlan, who was coaching at first, and tried to maul the Harlan coach for taunting him over allowing Jackson to get another homer. . . . [B]efore the two came to blows some of the other Harlan players stepped in as peacemakers, and the incident passed off without a bruise showing on either belligerent."

Williams held Standard to two singles, giving him eighteen consecutive scoreless innings in less than a week.

The *Evening Public Ledger* covered the losers' departure: "It was a downhearted assemblage of rooters, including the members of the company band, that crowded into North Philadelphia Station shortly after 6 o'clock on Saturday evening after Standard had lost this third game in succession to Harlan & Hollingsworth by 4–0 at the Phillies ball park."

As it turned out, Game 3 of the Atlantic Coast Shipyard Championship would be the sparkling jewel in the brief history of the DRSL.

The only World Series ever completed in September opened in Chicago on September 5, but only after baseball owners managed to persuade the War Department that the Red Sox and Cubs players should be exempt from the Work-or-Fight Order until the games were over. It was fully anticipated that the 1919 season would be canceled.

Due to wartime travel restrictions, it was decided that the first three games would be played in Chicago, and then the teams would move to Boston for whatever other games were necessary. Red Sox owner Harry Frazee protested the arrangement, noting that if the series were decided in four games, only one of them would be played in Boston. American League president Ban Johnson had harsh words for the Red Sox proprietor: "Some day Frazee will learn that the United States is engaged in a desperate war, the winning of which is the only thing that matters to the American public," he told the *Chicago Tribune*. The Cubs decided to use Comiskey Park, rather than their own Weeghman Park (later named Wrigley Field), on the theory that the larger White Sox stadium would bring in more money. To show their patriotic sides, and to stimulate attendance, the owners cut ticket prices in half. It didn't help: Attendance never exceeded twenty-eight thousand.

The Red Sox would eventually win the series in six games; it was their fourth championship in seven years—and their last for eighty-six years.

It was Babe Ruth's closing act as a pitcher, and he was superb. Boston won Game 1 by a score of 1–0, as Ruth gave up only six hits. After the Cubs won Game 2 and the Sox took Game 3, the series moved to Boston. Until the Cubs scored in the eighth inning of Game 4, Ruth had pitched 29.2 scoreless World Series innings. Ruth's feat was marred somewhat by the fact that many of the Cubs' best hitters had left the team during the season for either military service or "essential employment." Ruth's record stood until the Yankees Edward "Whitey" Ford broke it in 1961—the same year that Roger Maris broke Ruth's single-season home-run record of sixty.

The Red Sox and the Cubs refused to take the field for Game 5. Major League Baseball (MLB) had just imposed a new rule that players on the second-, third-, and fourth-place teams in each league would get a share of the World Series earnings, thereby reducing the payouts to the Red Sox and the Cubs. The owners neglected to inform the players of the change, and when they found out just before Game 5, they were incensed.

According to the website This Great Game, "Ban Johnson, in a less-than-sober state, entered the clubhouses and lowered his booming voice upon the players to put their trivial differences in perspective; why cause a stir over a few hundred bucks when Americans were dying in Europe? The players, without entirely endorsing Johnson's state of being, nevertheless got his point and carried on; the payout to players in the 1918 World Series would be the lowest ever: $1,102 [per player] for the Red Sox, $671 for the Cubs. Game Five began an hour later than scheduled."

Only about fifteen thousand fans were on hand to watch the Red Sox win Game 6 and the World Series by a score of 2–1 on September 11. The sparse crowd was probably partly due to fears over the rapidly spreading Spanish flu. It was an unusual series for several reasons. The Red Sox scored a total of only nine runs over the six games, the lowest total ever for a series winner. Indeed, they were outscored by the Cubs, who managed ten runs. And neither Ruth nor anyone else hit a home run.

During the seventh-inning stretch of the first game of the World Series at Wrigley Field in Chicago, a band suddenly struck up a rousing version of "The Star-Spangled Banner." The sparse crowd, in a frenzy of patriotism, rose, and before long, Francis Scott Key's lyrics were surging out of their throats. The players, now accustomed to military ways through their marching and drilling in their efforts to circumvent their draft boards, removed their caps, came smartly to attention, and turned their attention to Old Glory. The *New York Times* captured the moment:

> As the crowd of 10,274 spectators—the smallest that has witnessed the diamond classic in many years—stood up to take their afternoon yawn, that has been the privilege and custom of baseball fans for many generations, the band broke forth to the strains of "The Star-Spangled Banner."
>
> The yawn was checked and heads were bared as the ball players turned quickly about and faced the music. Jackie Fred Thomas of the U.S. Navy was at attention, as he stood erect, with his eyes set on the flag fluttering at the top of the lofty pole in right field. First, the song was taken up by a few, then others joined, and when the final notes came, a great volume of melody rolled across the field. It was at the very end that the onlookers exploded into thunderous applause and rent the air with a cheer that marked the highest point of the day's enthusiasm.

The performance was repeated the next day, and when the series moved to Boston, the Red Sox had the anthem played to open the game just before the traditional shout of "Play ball!" Although in the ensuing years there were sporadic instances of the song opening Major League games, it did not become a regular feature until World War II.

Just a few months before the 1918 World Series, Congressman John Charles Linthicum, a Maryland Democrat, had introduced legislation to make Key's song the national anthem, but it failed to win passage because of competition from other songs, including "Hail, Columbia," "My Country, 'Tis of Thee," and "America the Beautiful." Indeed, "The Star-Spangled Banner" would not win that designation until 1931.

With the Major League season over and the Work-or-Fight Order looming, the nation's shipyards and steel mills became hotbeds of cold feet. "With five weeks of idle time on their hands, the Major League players calmly proceeded to unite with whatever little teams would pay them any money, and the athletes, working at 'essential' trades five days a week, have been capering before delighted crowds on Saturdays and Sundays," said *Baseball Magazine*. The process was galvanized, not that it needed it, on September 12, when the draft age was expanded to include men ages eighteen to forty-five.

When Red Sox pitcher Carl Mays retired Cubs left fielder Les Mann on a groundout to second base to end the 1918 World Series, Ruth was confronted by the need to find "essential work" or face the military draft. Perhaps because his World Series check had been pared down to $1,100 by the owners' decision to spread the wealth with other teams, he decided that he first needed to capitalize on his heroic status and make some extra money to reconcile his gross habits with his net income. He turned to barnstorming.

Throughout the first half of the twentieth century, barnstorming was a big part of baseball players' lives. The term originally referred to itinerant theatrical companies who often performed in barns. Baseball players were paid from opening day until the end of the season. Even the highest-paid players had difficulty making ends meet in the off-season. Major League players were especially well received in cities that did not have big league teams. The practice endured until 1962, when a team led by Willie Mays staged an unsuccessful barnstorming tour.

The night of the World Series finale, Ruth served as the official starter at motorcycle races at Revere Beach, five miles north of Boston. Two days later, he was in New Haven, Connecticut, stationed at first base for the New Haven Colonials, a semiprofessional team, playing against the Cuban Stars, which was composed of players from the Negro Leagues. Ruth hit a home run, but his team lost, 5–1. That night, he was driven to Hartford, where he was given sumptuous accommodations at the swanky Bond Hotel. The next afternoon, he was pitching and batting third for the Hartford Polis, a semiprofessional club sponsored by Poli's Theater. He allowed only four hits in pitching a complete game shutout against the Fisk Red Tops of Chicopee, Massachusetts. The opposing pitcher was Dutch Leonard, his former Red Sox teammate, who gave up only one run. The sole run was driven in by Sam Agnew, Ruth's Red Sox batterymate. At the plate, Ruth had two hits, including a double off the Bull Durham tobacco sign in center field. Some five thousand fans watched the action.

Ruth was back in Hartford the following weekend to play in a doubleheader for the Polis. In the first game, he was locked in another pitchers' duel with a Red Sox teammate, Joe Bush, only this time, he was on the losing end of a 1–0 score. In the second game, the Polis faced an army team from Fort Slocum, New York. Five Major Leaguers, including Ruth, appeared that day. Behind the pitching of Ray Fisher, a New York Yankee, the soldiers defeated the Polis, 5–1. Ruth played first base and recorded a hit. Some three thousand were in attendance, most of them to see a doubleheader with Ruth.

How much Ruth was paid for these games cannot be determined, but the estimate for the first game in Hartford ranges from \$350 to \$1,300—the latter figure, of course, exceeding his World Series take. But sportswriter Joe S. Jackson of the *Detroit News* was reduced to sarcasm: "What work, if any Ruth is doing, no one seems to know. The Poli team must look like essential employment to him, it being reported that he was paid \$1,300, which is more than his world series bit for a game at Hartford one week previous. Last Sunday's double-header was for a war charity, but most folks would have to be shown the statement before being convinced that all these athletes journeyed to Hartford just to show that their hearts are in the right place."

In the week after the World Series, Ruth weighed offers from shipyards, steel mills, and munitions factories from all over the nation. His teammates—George Whiteman, Hank Miller, Jack Coffey, and George Cochran—all got draft-proof jobs. Ruth finally settled on Lebanon, probably at the urging of Agnew, who had caught both of his World Series games and was already there. Ruth was twenty-two years old and had hit only 21 of his 714 career home runs.

Eight days after the World Series ended, Ruth was at the Bethlehem Steel mill in Lebanon, negotiating with Pop Kelchner, the baseball coach and future super-scout for the Major Leagues.

He left town that same day, but he was back on September 23, with his wife, Helen, and stayed at a local hotel. The couple was seen dining with Agnew and his wife. It was the last time anyone remembered seeing Helen in Lebanon, and it is believed that she returned to the couple's eighty-acre farm home near Boston. Two days later, Ruth accepted a job at the plant. He told a Boston sportswriter, "It looks as though it's hard work all winter for me. All the boys have gone to work at some essential occupation and of course I'm big enough to do my bit. Before it's all over, I may be 'over there' yet."

Ruth's job title was "blueprint runner." His salary was reported to be $500 a week, which would be the equivalent of about $5,000 today. Whatever the amount, Ruth immediately celebrated his windfall by buying a 1918 Scripps-Booth roadster from a local dealer.

The next day's *Harrisburg Telegraph* was headlined, "Good Night! Lebanon Gets Babe Ruth." The *Harrisburg Patriot* said that the area was lucky to land the "Demon Slugger." The *Baltimore Sun* was pleased that Ruth had decided to "settle down in the small town of Lebanon for the winter." Noting that the regular Steel League season was over and that only exhibition games remained, a Lebanon sportswriter said, "Although little will be done in baseball at the Lebanon plant this year, it can easily be seen that the outfit will be on deck with a smash when the Industrial league season of 1919 is declared open."

Kelchner was working to build a strong team for 1919 to reclaim the BSL title Lebanon had lost to Steelton that fall. Other big leaguers joined Ruth on the Lebanon roster, including catcher Steve O'Neill (Indians), catcher Ducky Hale (Browns), second baseman Del Pratt (Yankees), third baseman Mike Mowrey (ex-Pirates), and pitcher Jess Buckles (ex-Yankees). No one knew, of course, that the war would be over in two months and that there would be a Major League season in 1919. Kelchner was unsuccessful in his attempts to lure future Hall of Famer George Sisler from the St. Louis Browns.

There was every expectation that Ruth would be in the lineup on Saturday, September 28, when the Lebanon nine took on a team of all-stars in an off-season exhibition. That night, the *Lebanon Evening Report* predicted, "There are few baseball fans in the city who will not be at Third and Green Streets tomorrow afternoon to see Manager Maurer's Lebanon Steel Leaguers offer battle to the speedy club managed by Jim Nasium and which includes big league stars." Jim Nasium was the pen name of Edgar Forrest Wolfe, a sportswriter and cartoonist from Philadelphia.

In the practice sessions leading up to the game, Ruth hit several home runs. In addition, Kelchner recalled, "One morning Babe broke up a practice session with his fungo hitting [hitting a ball that you toss yourself]. Every time he hit the ball it went out of the park with the result that we were soon without baseballs and practice for that morning had to cease. Later on, I discovered that there were scores of his admirers outside the park to whom he had promised baseballs, and he chose this means of supplying them!"

When the big game got underway, Ruth was playing first base. Scott Perry struck Ruth out the first two times he came to the plate. Lebanon's hurler, Ralph Stroud (ex-Yankees), held the all-stars hitless until the seventh inning. Ruth came to bat for the third time in the eighth inning, with the score tied, 2–2. Lebanon had men on second and third with nobody out. Perry intentionally walked Ruth. A groan went up from the 1,500 spectators as the unhittable pitches sailed by the future Sultan of Swat. But it was a wise strategy, for it set up a force out at any base and the possibility of a double play. Perry struck out the next three batters, and the all-stars went on to win, 4–2.

It was the only game Ruth would play for Lebanon. The following week, Lebanon went up against Traylor Ship, and although he was visiting his old home in Baltimore, Ruth was expected to return and be in the lineup. Lebanon trimmed Traylor, 5–0. Most of its Major League stars played. Ruth did not.

While writing an article on the BSL for the *Philadelphia Inquirer Magazine* in 1987, this author interviewed two men with firsthand knowledge of Ruth's time in Lebanon.

Ralph W. Clemens's modest home was a couple of miles from the old Bethlehem Steel mill in Lebanon. He umpired semiprofessional baseball games for most of his life, and by the time we met, his alert, octogenarian eyes still seemed ready to call a close one at first base. "I was seventeen, almost eighteen when Ruth was here. My father used to umpire the games over at Third and Green. I remember one game when my father was umpiring and Babe Ruth was playing first base. There was a pitcher that day who struck Ruth out twice. His name was . . ."— his power of recall seemed overtaken, but then it rallied—". . . was Scott Perry. That was it. He was really on that day. He struck Ruth out twice."

When Clemens was asked why Ruth and other ballplayers were working in steel mills and shipyards, his salt-and-pepper eyebrows dove to his nose in a frown: "Why, the whole gang of them was draft dodgers. They were supposed to be working for the war, but they didn't do any work. All they did was play baseball. Babe Ruth used to show up at the plant for an hour before practice. He'd be wearing fancy trousers, silk shirts, and patent-leather shoes. He just walked around talking to people about baseball. There wasn't anything essential about what he was doing."

Harris B. Light was twelve years old when he was the bat boy for the Lebanon mill team. He was smoking a cigar that had an ash hanging precariously from its parent leaf as he recalled, "You know, I remember one day the Babe said to me, 'Kid, I'm gettin' out of baseball and goin' into professional wrestling. There's a lot more money in it.'"

He said that Ruth had a girlfriend in nearby Myerstown and bought her a fur coat at a local store. He also said that Ruth left town without paying a huge bill to a butcher in Lebanon. "Ruth had a job in the plant. I think it was blueprint messenger. That's it. Blueprint messenger. . . ."

Then, Light cupped his ear. "What's that?" He echoed the question. "Were they dodging the draft?" He removed the cigar from his mouth to make room for astonishment. "Hell, yes! When the war ended and they all left town, I think Bethlehem Steel was glad to see them go so they didn't have to replace all those broken brooms from the big leaguers leaning on them."

He chuckled appreciatively at his own humor.

Cyril Hedricks, who was sixteen when Ruth came to Lebanon, worked at the steel mill. He gave this appraisal of the ballplayers in a 1981 interview: "They were slackers. They worked to get out of the draft. They didn't want to go in the war. They'd come walking in wearing their Sunday clothes, and then go off and read the newspaper somewhere. I didn't see them work."

The Lebanon County Historical Society has a "Babe Ruth" file, and among other things, it contains a Bethlehem Steel employee card issued to "Ruth, George 'Babe.'" It lists his eyesight as merely "good," and to the question, "Use Intoxicants?," the answer is "no."—a response that would have elicited guffaws from anyone who knew Ruth's habits. Indeed, behind his back, he was sometimes referred to as the Sultan of Sot. The card shows that Ruth was on the mill's payroll from September 25, 1918, to February 28, 1919. The society also has a grainy photograph of the Lebanon team with Ruth standing third from the left, looking as though he had been weaned on a lemon. It also has a uniform, which it says he may have worn. It's gray with blue striping and "Beth Steel" in red letters on the chest. There is no number.

Ruth was in Reading the next day, Sunday, September 29, for a rare convergence of superstars. He played on the Reading Steel Casting (RSC) team with Joe Jackson and Rogers Hornsby in a game against the old Harlan team of the Shipyard League, which brought its full ensemble of Major Leaguers, minus Jackson and Williams. About eighteen thousand fans, some of them lined five deep along the foul lines, watched the home team defeat Harlan, 6–5, in ten innings. Hundreds of others watched the game from housetops. Ruth pitched and played first base, but he didn't do well at the plate because he had been spiked the day before in Lebanon by Wally Schang. However, he relieved Williams in the fifth inning and shut Harlan out for the rest of the game. Reading scored the winning run when Pratt singled and went to second on a wild pickoff attempt by Dumont. Jackson hit a line drive that was knocked down by Dumont, who then threw wildly to first base, allowing Pratt to cross the plate. Jackson hit a home run in the first inning. M. G. Moore, the president of RSC, presented him with a crisp $20 bill at the end of the game. Hornsby went hitless.

The following weekend, Lebanon played the Traylor Shop team from the Shipyard League. The *Lebanon Daily News* speculated that

Ruth would play even though he had gone to Baltimore, probably to clear up the affairs of his father, who had died in August. But Ruth failed to show up. While in Baltimore, he claimed to have contracted the Spanish flu. The *Baltimore Sun* headlined, "Spanish 'Flu' Knocks Out Babe Ruth." He also missed Lebanon's last game of the year on October 12, when Lebanon lost to a team of Red Sox all-stars, 1–0. Red Sox ace Bush pitched the shutout, and Hornsby struck out four times.

Ruth was next in action on November 10, playing for the Baltimore Dry Docks team against the Nick Altrock all-stars. He hit two home runs in batting practice but managed only a double and single in the game, which the all-stars won, 5–4, in ten innings. Ruth injured his knee in the fourth inning while sliding home, catching his spikes on the plate. He stayed in the game, but he hobbled. That week, he returned to Lebanon on crutches and was confined to his apartment, unable to fulfill his duties as blueprint messenger at the steel mill.

As Ruth was journeying from Baltimore to Lebanon to recuperate on November 11, stunningly good news came—the war was over. An armistice was signed at the eleventh hour of the eleventh day of the eleventh month, ending the hostilities. Soon after, with the draft no longer menacing, Ruth headed back to join his wife at his farm in West Sudbury, some twenty miles west of Boston. Ruth had bought the farm so he could live as "a New England country gentleman." There, according to one account, he "cavorted gleeful as a puppy." Nevertheless, he stayed on the Bethlehem Steel payroll for another three months.

Ruth was back in his Red Sox uniform for the 1919 season and had a sensational year. His twenty-nine home runs set a new Major League record, and he led the league with 114 runs batted in (RBIs). He played some one hundred games in the outfield and also compiled a 9–5 pitching record. But on January 5, 1920, the Red Sox sold Ruth's rights to the New York Yankees for $125,000 (about $2.5 million today, still a bargain in today's baseball player market).

Ruth had now eclipsed Ty Cobb as baseball's premier attraction. He was finished as a pitcher, and with his sweeping, powerful, flawless swing, he would re-create the national pastime in his image. He would become the greatest hero in the history of American sports—and a genuine American legend.

It would be unfair to single Ruth out as a draft dodger, especially in light of the fact that many Major Leaguers who were in military uniforms had cushy stateside jobs as players or coaches. Then, there's the testimony of those soldiers abroad who found comfort and distraction in reports of his home runs and exploits on the field, not to mention whatever entertainment he provided the actual workers in the yards he played in. But it is accurate to say that his actions during the war were less than heroic.

Consider the experience of baseball players during World War II. Ted Williams spent three years as a Navy pilot—and lost two more prime seasons serving in the Korean conflict. Bob Feller did his pitching against the Japanese forces, Joe DiMaggio turned in his Yankee pinstripes for an army sergeant's stripes, and Hank Greenberg spent five prime years in the army. Ironically, though, when Japanese soldiers wanted to taunt Americans on the battlefield, their ultimate insult was to shout "To hell with Babe Ruth!" Ruth didn't have to fight to stand out as a symbol of the United States.

Besides, all the Major Leaguers who played for Lebanon, not just Ruth, left town right after the armistice. The *Lebanon News* lamented, "The base ball public will begin to see that the players merely used the steel mills and the ship yards as a shield for their personal ambitions. They merely accepted so-called essential occupations so that they might follow the work of their choosing, base ball. In most of the plants, the majors who were members of the representative base ball team did not do a day's work in a week, they were merely kept on the payroll for their ability to play the diamond game."

As soon as Hornsby's Fort Worth draft board informed him that he had been reclassified as 1-A in June, the slugging shortstop contacted the management of Harlan & Hollingsworth in Wilmington. He probably knew of the draft-proof shipyard from all the publicity generated by Jackson's move there in May. In mid-July, he received an offer of employment as a boilermaker, and he told Harlan that he would be ready to go to work at the end of the Major League season. Hornsby had a subpar season with the Cardinals, who finished thirty-three games behind the pennant-winning Cubs.

On September 5, five days after the regular season ended, Hornsby was in Wilmington, filling out paperwork for his new job. One report set his salary at $400 per month. He was joined by Bob Steele, a New York Giants pitcher. That night, the two ballplayers traveled to Reading, where they were escorted around town by M. G. Moore, the president of RSC. "And both met a number of the local baseball followers," according to the *Reading Times.* On September 10, Hornsby was back in Wilmington, where he made his Harlan debut in a game against a team from Hopewell, Virginia. He drove in two runs in his first at-bat and made several slick plays in the field.

Hornsby made his first appearance with RSC on September 15. His team swamped the R. G. Dun & Company team from Philadelphia, 19–1. Hornsby, Jackson, and Pratt each hit home runs. Seven of the nine Reading starters were active Major Leaguers. Jackson also threw out a runner at home plate. Hornsby played shortstop.

The day after the one-sided game, the *Reading Times* promised, "No more joke teams will be sent against the all-star cast, which now is one of the best in the country. A mistake was made in booking inferior clubs to oppose the local stars, and as a result, some of the games were more or less of a joke." The next game would be against the Fourth Naval District team, which had several former Major Leaguers on its roster.

There was a major buildup for a September 21 game in which Harlan would play a team from Cramp's Shipyard. But with 2,500 fans awaiting, the Cramp's team failed to show up. To placate the fans, Harlan played an intrasquad game—Payne's Pets versus Gallagher's Gallopers. Hornsby and Jackson played on the Pets, and each had two hits. Both teams' rosters were dominated by active Major Leaguers. In addition to Hornsby and Jackson, the participants in the pickup game included Lee Dressen (Tigers), Joe Lake (ex-Tigers), George Dumont (Senators), Bob Steele (Giants), Gus Getz (Pirates), Ed Gharrity (Senators), Zinn Beck (Yankees), Harry Biemiller (future Reds), and Fred Payne (ex–White Sox).

There was, in fact, a reason Cramp's was a no-show: The whole shipyard was on strike to protest the special treatment accorded baseball players.

No one provided a bigger postseason shelter for big league ballplayers than the venerable Cramp's Shipyard in Philadelphia, which was excluded from the DRSL because it wasn't owned by Bethlehem Steel. Cramp's, founded in 1830, had become world famous some ten years earlier because it built most of President Theodore Roosevelt's "Great White Fleet," the group of navy battleships that circumnavigated the globe between 1907 and 1909. Most fighting ships were painted gray to be less visible, but Roosevelt ordered these to be white to display America's naval power to the world.

By September 10, 1918, no fewer than a dozen Major Leaguers had made their way to Cramp's: Red Sox catcher Wally Schang (twenty-nine years old in 1918), Red Sox pitcher Joe Bush (age twenty-five), Tigers shortstop Owen "Donie" Bush (age thirty),

Reds outfielder Sherwood Magee (age thirty-four), Phillies pitcher Erskine Mayer (age twenty-nine), and seven players from the Athletics roster—pitcher John "Mule" Watson (age twenty-two), catcher James "Wickey" McAvoy (age twenty-four), outfielder Charlie Jamieson (age twenty-five), outfielder Reuben "Rube" Oldring (age thirty-four), pitcher Scott Perry (age twenty-seven), and outfielder Jake Munch (age twenty-seven).

But on September 20, some two thousand Cramp's workers—boilermakers, riveters, and reamers—staged a one-day strike to protest the shipyard's policy of giving the baseballers easier jobs and higher salaries than they had. They also said that the ballplayers "c[ame] and [went] as they please[d]." Whenever a journalist asked a striker why he had walked off the job, the standard reply was "It's not what you know, it's who you know." After leaving the shipyard, the strikers met at a hall and said that they wanted to go before a U.S. Senate investigating committee and testify that players for the local Phillies and the Athletics, plus the champion Red Sox, had been given soft jobs so they could escape the draft and the shipyard would have a good baseball team the following year.

Cramp's executives retorted that the workers were trying to excuse their own underproductivity by blaming it on the baseball players. The *New York Tribune* tossed a log on that fire by editorializing, "Ball players who go to work in grimy, sooty shipyards, riding in automobiles and dressed in clothes that would be more appropriate in the lobby of a $9 a day hotel, may not be efficient workmen, but according to some of the shipyard executives, the ball players can learn much in the way of slacking by careful observation of the 'skilled workmen.'"

Labor leaders at Hog Island, under fire for lagging production, blamed baseball players for not doing enough work. They singled out such players as Pep Young (age twenty-nine), a Detroit Tigers second baseman, who "had nothing to do except watch other men work. . . . [They] didn't know a bolt from a screw." However, they said that Chief Bender was always at work and did more labor than his crew.

The war ended before the Senate could look into the workers' grievances.

On September 23, Hornsby was in Philadelphia, where he married his childhood sweetheart, Sarah Evelyn Martin. Both the bride and the groom were twenty-two years old. The Hornsbys spent part of their honeymoon in Reading as guests of M. G. Moore. Under the headline "Hornsby to Make Home in Reading," the *Reading Times* of October 10 noted that Hornsby and his new wife "[we]re now quartered in the Berkshire hotel and they expect to go to housekeeping." It cited this development as incontrovertible evidence that "the Reading Steel Casting Company has already started building up its base ball team for the 1919 season."

The *Reading Eagle* said, "Hornsby is securing work at the local plant of the Bethlehem Steel Corporation, has moved his belongings here, and is living at the Berkshire Hotel." That same day, the *Lebanon Daily News* reported that Hornsby "[wa]s to become a member of the Lebanon Bethlehem Steel League team in 1919."

It seems that Hornsby intended to play for Lebanon on Saturdays and Reading on Sundays in 1919.

Although the Great War would end on November 11, even as late as October, it was widely assumed that the 1919 Major League season would be canceled because it would still be wartime. Indeed, American League president Johnson ordered that league's season scratched. The Steel and Shipyard Leagues fully expected to be operating in 1919 with their Major League players. Fearing financial losses in 1919, the big league owners released all of their remaining players at the end of the 1918 season.

But then, suddenly, the war was over. Although he remained on the Bethlehem Steel payroll until February 1919, Ruth was back at his farm near Boston, where he wintered and prepared to return to the Red Sox. Jackson was at home with his wife in Greenville, South Carolina. Hornsby was back in Fort Worth with his new bride. And dozens of other Major Leaguers, who had gone to the steel mills and shipyards, would leave Pennsylvania and Delaware to return to their homes and their Major League careers. This exodus only reinforced the widespread belief that they had been allowed to play baseball instead of serving in the military.

By the end of the war, twenty-four million men had registered for the draft. Some 2.7 million of them served in the military, including about 250 active Major Leaguers. About 112,000 of them would be killed, including eight current or former big leaguers.

By early 1919, MLB was ready for a new season. All the players who had been released the previous September, now nominally free agents, were nevertheless signed back with their original teams. However, an elephant remained in the room—what to do with the men who had played for the steel mills and shipyards.

E. W. Dickerson, president of the Central League and a member of the National Board of Professional Leagues, was unstinting: "Players of professional baseball who have gone into occupations during the war enabling them to dodge patriotic war service should be blacklisted in organized baseball for all time. They are little better than traitors, and will never again play in any organization with which I am connected, if it is within my power to prevent it."

From Kentucky, the *Paducah Sun-Democrat* ran an editorial that was headlined "NO BASEBALL FOR SLACKERS" and read, "The sports-loving public will approve the suggestions that professional baseball players, who ran to cover in shipyards, to dodge the draft, be barred from the diamond forever. Baseball, as the national sport, has a clean record for manliness. 'Yellow' players are hissed from the game if they show the streak on the field. Then all the more reason that slackers who showed the yellow streak to their government be barred. No man of the right type could preserve his self-respect if thrown into contact with the slacker breed in as intimate a pursuit as baseball." The *El Paso Herald* added, "Those men were slackers, pure and simple, and should not be permitted to return to the game."

But the baseball magnates had little interest in damaging their product for a mere patriotic principle. White Sox owner Charles Comiskey, who seven months earlier had proclaimed, "There is no room on my club for players who wish to evade the draft by entering the employ of shipbuilders," welcomed Jackson and others back to his fold. Connie Mack in Philadelphia, Harry Frazee in Boston, Jake Ruppert in New York, Clark Griffith in Washington, and their counterparts in St. Louis, Cincinnati, Detroit, and Cleveland were similarly magnanimous.

However, a large group of industrial leaguers decided to hang up their spikes: Fred Anderson, Paddy Baumann, Johnny Beall, Earl Blackburn, Lee Dressen, Ed Fitzpatrick, Ducky Hale, Olaf Henriksen, Hugh High, Alex Main, Ed Miller, Ed Monroe, Mike Mowrey, George Pierce, and Jeff Tesreau all chose not to return to the Major Leagues.

Bethlehem Steel officials tried to keep their six-team baseball circuit going into 1919, but their star players, so eager to get on the steel and shipyard payrolls just a few months earlier, now were happily back with their American and National League teams.

On March 15, 1919, the *New York Times* carried a short item: "The Bethlehem Steel Baseball League, which was the haven of major league baseball players when the 'work-or-fight' order went into effect, has disbanded. The league has been in existence two years, and last year it attracted a number of big league players."

As American shipyards went through a postwar cycle of closings and downsizing, the DRSL faded out of existence in 1919.

Meanwhile, attendance doubled over the previous year in the 1919 Major League season.

7

THOSE WHO WENT—OVER THERE AND OVER HERE

> "I saw Christy Mathewson doomed to die. None of us who were with him at the time realized that the rider on the pale horse had passed his way. Nor did Matty. . . ."
>
> —Ty Cobb

Four future members of the Baseball Hall of Fame—Christy Mathewson, Ty Cobb, George Sisler, and Branch Rickey—volunteered for perilous duty, developing offensive chemical munitions and defending against poisonous gas attacks.

Indeed, the army said that the Chemical Warfare Service was the most dangerous placement it had. The official manual for the unit, which was dubbed the "Gas and Flame Division," said that the "flamemen" usually "go into action ahead of the attacking waves of infantry, carrying tanks on their backs, and advance under cover of artillery barrage squirting flames of liquid fire from the tanks." The "gas men" advance carrying "a sack of gas-filled bombs which they hurl into trenches and dugouts like grenades."

Mathewson (age thirty-seven) had won 372 games in a seventeen-year career as a pitcher, mostly with the New York Giants, placing him tied for third on the career victories list. Ironically, he would be tied with Pete Alexander, who also would have his baseball career and life damaged on the World War I battlefield.

Mathewson had an archival memory. Batters said that when they got a hit off Mathewson, they never saw the same pitch again.

His control was legendary. He once pitched sixty-eight consecutive innings without issuing a walk. In the 1904 World Series against the Philadelphia Athletics, Mathewson won three of the five Giants' victories. All were shutouts. He had an earned run average of 2.13 over seventeen seasons. He retired in 1916 and was managing the Cincinnati Reds when he joined the army on August 28, 1918. His enlistment was strongly opposed by his wife, Jane, who thought that he was too old for military duty.

But Mathewson persisted, deploying to France in September. He was commissioned as a captain and attached to the chemical unit. He was posted to Blois, then Tours, and finally Chaumont, about 150 miles southeast of Paris, where he joined Rickey.

Although he had a wife and four children, Rickey enlisted and was in France by August. During his weeklong voyage over the Atlantic, more than one hundred of his fellow soldiers aboard the ship succumbed to the Spanish flu. He got pneumonia and had to be carried ashore on a stretcher. Sisler was undergoing training in Virginia when the war ended and never joined his countrymen in France.

While he was still playing baseball in August, and his Tigers were in Washington for a series against the Senators, Cobb went to the War Department and applied for a commission in the Chemical Warfare Service. A week later, he was informed that he was now a captain in the U.S. Army and should report for duty by October 1. Cobb explained why he had chosen the riskiest duty of all: "The public has knocked baseball unmercifully. This knocking has been uncalled for. Anyone who calls me a slacker is dead wrong. That I am going in as a captain will be criticized, but none can say that I will be protected from danger more than the humblest private in the trenches. If I were a general, it might be different. As a captain I shall be in the same position as an enlisted man." Cobb asked for and received permission to skip basic training and go directly to France. He thought that basic training sounded too much like "spring training." Looking dapper in his well-tailored uniform, Captain Cobb embarked for France on October 6.

Cobb's patriotic manifestations inspired L. C. Davis, a *St. Louis Post-Dispatch* sportswriter who often turned poet:

Ty Cobb has joined the gas and flame;
When Ty gets in the fighting game
He'll make the Germans swear.
He'll steal up on the Huns in France
And steal the Kaiser's coat and pants
When he gets "over there."

He'll bat the Crown Prince from the box
And steal his hat and shoes and sox
And everything in sight.
When he gets in the fight.
He'll steal a march upon the Huns
And steal their mustard gas and guns
When he gets in the fight.

He'll steal a mile or two of trench
And put their Kaiser on the bench,
When he gets in the scrap.
He'll steal the watch upon the Rhine,
He'll steal Von Hindy's famous line
And wipe it off the map.

He'll lead the league in batting Huns,
He'll show those German sons-of-guns
They have no chance to win.

He'll go through villages and towns
Like going through the famous Browns
Until he hits Berlin.

In point of fact the Georgia Peach
A lesson to those Huns will teach
That they will not forget;
For cover they will quickly hike
When Tyrus Raymond starts to spike
Their guns already yet.

When Tyrus Raymond hits his stride
Unter den Linden he will slide
And score the winning run.
That famous battery Me und Gott
He'll hammer all around the lot
Until the game is won.

OVER THERE. Mustard gas—so-called because it smelled like mustard plants—was usually dispersed by bombs or artillery. Its presence was not immediately apparent, but within twenty-four hours, victims had intense itching and large blisters filled with yellow liquid that caused chemical burns. Mustard gas was seldom fatal, but it had the tactical effect of removing troops from the field because they required lengthy periods of convalescence.

By mid-October, the Germans were in retreat, and the Gas and Flame Division was given the seemingly routine task of teaching gas-mask techniques to a group of new recruits who would probably never need them. But the baseball trio had received only about one week of training in the subject they were teaching, and this was no ordinary group of recruits. They were deadbeats, hard cases, and rejects from other units. The army theorized that these men would listen to famous athletes like Mathewson, Cobb, and Rickey. Cobb described what happened:

> [W]e marched about eighty of our culls into a dark, air-tight chamber for practice. Real mustard gas was to be released right after a signal was given warning us to snap masks into place and file out in an orderly way. Then we were to dive into trenches as if under machine-gun fire. Well, the warning signal was poorly given and a lot of us missed it, including Christy Mathewson and me.
>
> Men screamed when they breathed a smell of death. Crazy with fear, they piled up to escape, a hopeless tangle of bodies. As soon as I realized what was happening, I fixed my mask . . . groped my way over to a wall, and worked toward the door. I fell outside . . . was damned lucky. Most of the poor bastards were trapped inside. When it was over there were sixteen bodies stretched out on the ground. Eight men died within hours of lung damage. In a few days, others were crippled.

Rickey was not affected, but Cobb had had enough exposure to the gas that he felt weak and had a persistent cough. Mathewson, however, was not so lucky: "Ty, I got a good dose of the stuff. I feel terrible."

By the time Mathewson got back to the United States in February 1919, his job managing the Reds had been taken. He served as a Giants coach from 1919 to 1921, but he was also in a death struggle with tuberculosis. He spent most of his time in Saranac Lake, New York, where he was treated at the renowned Trudeau Sanitarium. He died of tuberculosis there on October 7, 1925—nearly seven years to the day following his exposure at

Chaumont. He was forty-five years old. Most people, including Cobb, believed that the poisonous gas was a contributing factor to his early demise.

In addition to tying Mathewson for third place in career victories, Alexander is ranked tenth in innings pitched and second in shutouts in a twenty-year career with the Phillies, the Cubs, and the Cardinals. He had won more than thirty games in each of the three previous seasons when he was drafted into the army and reported for duty on April 27, 1918. "No one will have a chance to call me a slacker," he said. But malignant stars hovered when he arrived in France in June as part of the 342nd Field Artillery, Eighty-Ninth Division.

Sergeant Alexander took part in the St. Mihiel Offensive in September and the Meuse-Argonne Offensive from mid-October until the armistice. The percussive chorus of artillery rounds, punctuated by enormous shudders of sound, left him deaf in his left ear, and he had muscle damage in his right arm—his pitching arm—from pulling a lanyard to fire the howitzers. He also suffered what was then called shell shock but today is labeled post-traumatic stress disorder. Later, he became epileptic and an alcoholic. Baseball historian Jan Finkel suggests that one was the cause of the other: "Alex tried to cover up his epilepsy, using alcohol in the mistaken belief that it would alleviate the condition. Living in a world that believed epileptics to be touched by the devil, he knew it was more socially acceptable to be a drunk."

Alexander returned to the Cubs and, after a dismal start, resumed a successful pitching career that lasted into 1930. "Alcohol was taking over his life, as he drank to relieve the past, forget the present, and forestall the future," says Finkel. "No longer a great pitcher, he was still a very good one, capable of picking up 22 wins in 1923 and setting a major-league record by starting the season pitching 52 consecutive innings before issuing a walk."

Finkel writes that Alexander's retirement years were "the picture of a man spinning out of control with nobody able to stop the free-fall":

> Alex entered various sanitariums seeking help, but nothing worked. He was hooked. Having put up with enough, [wife] Amy divorced him in 1929, hoping to shock him to his senses. . . . Alex and Amy remarried in 1931. He shuffled around the country in an odyssey of odd jobs . . . cheap hotels, boarding houses, and the like. His poverty and inability to straighten out became an embarrassment to the National League. The Alexander file at the Hall of Fame contains a collection of letters exchanged among Commissioner Kenesaw Mountain Landis, National League president Ford Frick, Cardinal president Sam Breadon, and Cardinal general manager Branch Rickey—all of them addressing the question "What to do about Alexander?" They finally settled on the ruse of a National League pension of fifty dollars a month that was actually paid by the Cardinals and sent to whoever was keeping Alex to dole out to him as necessary. That, they hoped, with his small army pension, might keep Alexander from drowning.

He died on November 4, 1950. Jim Leeke writes in *The Best Team Over There: The Untold Story of Grover Cleveland Alexander and the Great War*, "Grover Cleveland Alexander, a sixty-three-year-old alcoholic, died alone in a rented room in St. Paul, Nebraska. Once he had been the most dominant pitcher in the National League. He had won 373 games during twenty seasons in the Major Leagues, trailing only Cy Young and Walter Johnson and tied with mighty Christy Mathewson. Schoolboys knew Alexander's record by heart."

Rickey, who led the front office of Alexander's Cardinals, said, "I doubt that I ever felt sorrier for any man who ever worked for me than I did for Alexander. He was a perfectly wonderful fellow and his only enemy was himself."

The 342nd Field Artillery Regiment, which included big leaguers and star athletes among its officers and men, fielded an outstanding baseball team. In addition to Alexander, the team included these active Major Leaguers: Otis Lambeth (age twenty-eight), Indians pitcher; Clarence Mitchell (age twenty-seven), Dodgers first baseman; Win Noyes (age twenty-nine), Athletics pitcher; and Charles Ward (age twenty-four), Dodgers shortstop.

In a letter to a friend, Lambeth said that if he had his choice between fighting in France or playing on a pennant-winning team, he would choose the former. And he wrote this to a Cleveland sportswriter: "Fritz has tried to shell me, to gas me, to bomb me, and I presume he is lying awake nights thinking of other means to obliterate me from this earth of ours. So far I have been spared and he has wasted a lot of powder trying to get me. And all the time we have been sending him a little better than he has handed us." And Lambeth, who had been born in Berlin, Kansas, said, "I don't want to die until I reach Berlin. I just want to see if they resemble each other in something else besides the name."

In a letter to Dodgers owner Charles Ebbets, Ward made this observation: "Baseball never did and never will have the thrills the big game had. A fellow going to sleep at night, if anything like sleep could be had, would remark in the morning, 'Well, boys, I am still in the game.' Charles, I could write more than one book on my experiences and close calls, but here I am, still in the ring. I wouldn't want to go through it again for millions, but wouldn't have missed it for thousands."

In another letter to Ebbets, Mitchell said that the troops were eager to get home: "We were told for our Christmas that we would be homeward bound in another month, so expect to be in time to start spring training the same as ever."

But getting home was no easy task. The army was unprepared for the sudden end of the war, and there were two million men in Europe and a logistical nightmare in organizing their return by ship. In fact, the last American combat unit did not leave France until January 1920—some fourteen months after the armistice. The army's preparations on the home front showed how little was understood about the toll the war had taken on soldiers like Alexander. The concern of the army brass was that the veterans would be disorderly or financial burdens.

The 342nd Field Artillery Regiment was stationed in Germany after the armistice, and no one knew when it would be ordered home. This uncertainty was especially difficult for the baseball players because spring training for the 1919 season was right around the corner. Back home, owners and managers also fretted about their missing players. Lambeth, Noyes, Mitchell, and Ward all sought early returns but were denied. The unit did not get back to the United States until May 27.

Lambeth did not get back to the Indians until 1919—and was promptly sent down to the minors, where he toiled for two years. The soldier who had said that he would rather fight in France than win a pennant never made it back to the Big Show. His hometown newspaper, the *Iola Register*, grumbled, "He has been 'bumped' out of the big league, given way to some shipyard working ball player or exempted man who played ball while he took part in several engagements in France."

Noyes was a promising spitballer with the Athletics, but he never regained his prewar form. In a very brief Major League career with the Athletics and the White Sox, he compiled a win-loss record of 11–15.

Ward returned to the Dodgers in July and played shortstop for five seasons, ending with a career batting average of .228. Mitchell's dubious distinction came in the 1920 World Series, when he hit a sharp line drive that was speared by Cleveland's second baseman

Bill Wambsganss, who turned it into an unassisted triple play—to this day, the only one in the October Classic. Mitchell set another World Series record the next time he came to bat when he hit into a double play—thereby becoming responsible for five outs in two consecutive plate appearances. In an eighteen-year career, Mitchell had a record of 125–139 as a pitcher and a batting average of .291.

Eddie Grant was a Harvard-educated ballplayer who began an eleven-year Major League career as a good-fielding-non-hitting infielder with four teams. (It was said that due to his Ivy League pedigree, Grant refused to say, "I got it," when going to a pop fly, preferring instead the more grammatically correct "I have it!") He used his baseball earnings to go to Harvard Law School, and he quit the Giants in 1915 and went into law practice. When the United States entered the war in 1917, Grant volunteered in hopes of becoming an army officer, but he told friends, "I had determined from the start to be in this war if it came to us, and if I am not successful in becoming an officer, I shall enlist as a private, for I believe there is no greater duty that I owe for being what I am—an American citizen."

He was commissioned as an infantry captain, assigned to the Seventy-Seventh Division, and soon was in the thickest fighting. During the Meuse-Argonne Offensive, a group of some five hundred Americans found themselves cut off from the rest of the army and surrounded by German troops. This was the famous "Lost Battalion." Grant's unit was battling to reach the trapped men on October 5, 1918. Late in the afternoon, Grant was struggling to stay awake after three sleepless days and nights. Lost sleep groped at his brain as he saw his commanding officer, Major Delancey Jay, being carried on a stretcher. Jay lifted his head, looked into Grant's eyes, and ordered, "Take command of the battalion!" Minutes later, Grant was struck by an artillery shell and killed instantly.

On Decoration Day, 1921, the Giants unveiled a monument to Grant at the Polo Grounds. It was later stolen, but the monument was replicated many years later at Oracle Park, home of the San Francisco Giants.

Six other former or active Major Leaguers died while on military duty.

The first was Ralph Sharman (age twenty-three), an Athletics outfielder, who drowned in a training accident at Camp Sheridan, Alabama, on May 24, 1918.

The next was Marcus Milligan (age twenty-two), a right-handed pitcher who had been signed by the Pittsburgh Pirates in 1916 but never got in a game. He was killed while training in a Curtiss JN-4 "Jenny" two-seat biplane, which crashed near Barron Field in Fort Worth on September 4, 1918.

Alex Burr, who had played in one game for the Yankees in 1914, was killed in a mid-air collision while on a training exercise at Cazaux, France, some thirty-five miles southwest of Bordeaux, on October 12, 1918. It was his twenty-fifth birthday.

Robert "Bun" Troy (age thirty), a right-handed pitcher who had played in one game for the Tigers, died in Petit Maujouy, France, on October 7, 1918, of wounds suffered in combat. He was a sergeant in the Eightieth Division and had been born in Germany.

Newt Halliday (age twenty-two), who had played first base for the Pirates in 1916, died on April 6, 1918, at the Great Lakes Naval Station. The official cause of his death was tuberculosis and acute pneumonia.

Larry Chappell (age twenty-eight), a lefthanded outfielder who had played for the White Sox, the Indians, and the Braves in a four-year career that ended in 1917, died of the Spanish flu on November 8, 1918, while serving in the Army Medical Corps at Letterman General Hospital in San Francisco.

Harry Glenn (age twenty-eight), a catcher who had played with the Cardinals in 1915, was training as an aviation mechanic in the Army Signal Corps in St. Paul, Minnesota, when he developed pneumonia and died on October 12, 1918.

OVER THERE. Pearl "Specks" Webster (age twenty-nine) played catcher and first base in the Negro Leagues, including several seasons with the Brooklyn Royal Giants. He was drafted and sent to France with the 807th Pioneer Infantry Regiment and saw action in the Meuse-Argonne Offensive. He contracted the Spanish flu on November 10 and died on November 16, five days after the armistice. In 1952, Webster was named to a list of the "Greatest Black Players" by the *Pittsburgh Courier*.

Leeke estimates that sixty active and former Major League Baseball (MLB) players served in the American Expeditionary Force. Many of them displayed courage, a few were wounded, and three—Grant, Troy, and Burr—died there.

The first active big leaguer to enlist in the military was Hank Gowdy, who signed up on June 1, 1917, at the age of twenty-eight. Gowdy, a lifetime .270 hitter, played catcher and occasionally first base for the Braves and the Giants in a seventeen-year career. He was the hero of the Braves' upset win over the Athletics in the 1914 World Series. He arrived in France in March 1918 and fought in the trenches against the German spring offensive. He received a hero's welcome when he returned to Boston.

Playing for the Giants in 1924, Gowdy became a World Series goat when, in the twelfth inning of the seventh game, Washington's Herold "Muddy" Ruel hit a pop-up. Gowdy tore off his catcher's mask and looked skyward. Then, he stepped on said mask and, thus encumbered, was unable to catch the ball. Ruel promptly doubled and then scored the Senators' winning run. Sportswriters, subtracting the losers' World Series share from the winners', pronounced it the $50,000 muff.

During World War II, Gowdy rejoined the army as a major at the age of fifty-four and became chief athletic officer at Fort Benning, Georgia.

In a playing career between 1904 and 1912 with the Reds, the Senators, and the Yankees, catcher Charles "Gabby" Street (age thirty-five) had a batting average of .208. He was, however, far more successful after the war as manager of the Cardinals, whom he led to two pennants (1930 and 1931) and one World Series victory in 1931.

Street enlisted in March 1918, intending to go to France. He told *The Sporting News*: "I was sent to Fort Slocum, N.Y., and everybody interested in baseball thought it was great that I should be on hand to catch the army team. I finally convinced my lieutenant that I joined the army to fight, pointing out that I could have continued playing baseball for a salary." As a member of the First Gas Regiment, Chemical Warfare Division, Street participated in three major engagements—Chateau Thierry, St. Mihiel, and the Meuse-Argonne Offensive. He was awarded the Purple Heart after being shot in his right leg by a German airplane gunner.

Right-hander Elmer Ponder (age twenty-five) pitched for the Pirates and the Cubs before and after the war. He served as an army aviator and won the French Cross for valor. According to the *Baltimore Sun*, Ponder shot down two German planes over the summer and another near the end of the war and received the designation of "ace."

Tom Quinlan (age thirty) played outfield for the Cardinals and the White Sox between 1913 and 1915. Three days before the armistice, and a few days after he had been sent to the front lines, he was wounded by a German artillery shell. No medics were available, and Quinlan was forced to walk a mile to the nearest field station, where medics rushed him to a mobile hospital. There surgeons amputated his right arm and removed his left eye.

Three Major Leaguers were injured in gas attacks that led to early deaths. Charlie Becker (age twenty-seven), former Washington Senators pitcher, died at thirty-seven. Oran Dodd (age twenty-seven), infielder with the Giants, died at thirty-eight. Marsh Williams (age twenty-five), Philadelphia Athletics pitcher, died at forty-two.

Leon Cadore, Dodgers pitcher, was commissioned as a lieutenant and was one of the white officers assigned to the 369th Infantry Regiment, which was composed of black soldiers known as "the Harlem Hellfighters." The unit distinguished itself in the final days of the war by capturing nearly a thousand German troops. In gratitude, the French government awarded the 369th the Croix de Guerre. Cadore was unstinting in his praise for his troops: "Every man in my regiment fought with the courage of a lion."

Cadore returned to the Dodgers in 1919 and pitched for several teams before retiring in 1924. On May 1, 1920, he was locked in a pitchers' duel with Joe Oeschger of the Boston Braves. The game went on for twenty-six innings—the highest number in Major League history—and both pitchers went the distance. The game was called after batters complained that they could no longer see the ball. Cadore estimated that he had thrown three hundred pitches and said that he couldn't comb his hair for three days. It took three hours and fifty minutes to complete the game, which was nearly three games in one. Today's average nine-inning game takes about three hours. The second-longest game—the White Sox versus the Brewers in 1984—took eight hours and six minutes.

Joe Jenkins (age twenty-seven) was a bullpen catcher for the White Sox in 1917 when he was drafted into the army. He arrived in France in the spring of 1918 to join the 132nd Infantry Regiment and saw action in Flanders, St. Mihiel, and the Argonne.

The regiment was heavily populated by White Sox fans, and in a letter to Charles Comiskey, Jenkins wrote:

> We have been scrapping for the past ten days on the Meuse, north of Verdun, and believe me the fighting has been hot and sharp. It is becoming more apparent that Germany is through. . . . I am with the One Hundred and Thirty-second regiment, which is commanded by Col. Davis of Chicago, and most of the men in my platoon are from the south side, and their favorite spot is the left field of the bleachers. Believe me, those south siders can go some. . . . Give my regards to all the boys and tell them that in this league over here the pitchers all have plenty on everything that they throw.

Jenkins's bravery under fire earned him a commission as a first lieutenant.

He returned to the White Sox in 1919 and was present for, although not involved in, the Black Sox scandal. More than forty years later, he told an interviewer, "We players who weren't involved in the payoff thought things were funny in that first game in Cincinnati. We should have beaten Cincinnati blindfolded. We had everything, the hitters, the pitchers, the power and the speed. . . . Yes, it was a terrible mess."

Mike Menosky (age twenty-three) was an outfielder for the Senators when he got the call from his draft board in Flint, Michigan. He saw action in France as an infantryman and returned to the Senators for the 1919 season. The Senators traded Menosky to the Red Sox, who were looking for a replacement in the outfield for Babe Ruth, who had departed for the Yankees. Menosky gave the Boston fans the best year of his career, hitting .297 and driving in sixty-four runs. Ruth, however, batted .378, with fifty-four home runs and 135 runs batted in (RBIs).

Hughie Miller (age thirty-one) was a veteran minor leaguer who had played one game at first base for the Phillies in 1911. As soon as America declared war in April 1917, Miller enlisted in the Marine Corps and moved to the trenches in March 1918. Miller had been hospitalized with a high fever just before the Americans counterattacked the Germans at Belleau Wood on June 6, 1918. Ignoring the pleas of physicians, Miller hooked up with his platoon, which soon was under heavy machine-gun fire. He captured two German soldiers single-handedly, and a week later General John Pershing himself presented Miller with the Distinguished Service Cross for his "extraordinary heroism."

Miller was shot in the shoulder on July 18 at the Battle of Soissons and hospitalized for a month. He was wounded again on September 12 at the Battle of Saint-Mihiel when a bomb exploded near him.

Miller returned to the United States in January 1919 on the same troop ship as Lieutenant Colonel Cap Huston, part-owner of the Yankees. Several newspapers reported that Huston was "going to urge his colleagues in the big show to take steps toward caring for ballplayers who were disabled in the war. He believes the club owners would provide employment for all such players and mentioned Hugh Miller."

It never happened.

In December 1918, *Baseball Magazine*, ever the ardent cheerleader for the national pastime, ran an editorial that seemed to suggest that MLB players had defeated Germany almost single-handedly:

> All around the circuits, great ballplayers went to war after the season closed. Most of them slipped into uniform so quietly that the public never heard of it till weeks after they enlisted. There was no shirking, there was no slacking. The athletes

> simply declared themselves in on the war, got measured for khaki suits, and vanished into the cantonments. If an accurate census of the various clubs could have been taken around October 20th, it would have shown so large a percentage of the players serving Uncle Sam that the knockers would have been dumbfounded forever. Practically every unmarried man among the big leaguers had gone reported for war; many of the married men had followed suit, and every man in the whole array, not in the actual khaki or blue, had found some thoroughly essential occupation. Find a dodger, a slacker, or a shirker in baseball, under Government rules—you can't do it. The only ballplayers under suspicion were those who, in mid-season, had skipped to the Safe Shelter League, the haven of the shipyards and munition plants. Many of the older players went into the shipyards AFTER September 1—and there is a world of difference between these fellows, who went in after the season was practically over, with no thought of getting extra money by playing ball, and the guys who skidded under cover in June or July, thinking of safety from the trenches and sweet deals for entertaining crowds on the diamond.

Leeke estimates that several hundred active Major Leaguers were in military uniforms in November 1918. However, the majority of them did their service "over here," and many of them merely played baseball and entertained the troops. The U.S. Navy was far and away the ballplayers' preferred branch, and they were rewarded with duties that took advantage of their strongest skill. Here are a few examples of—to borrow *Baseball Magazine*'s phrase—big leaguers "gone to war."

Pitcher Burleigh Grimes was traded to the Dodgers in 1917 and enlisted in the navy during the 1918 season. He was assigned to a recruiting station in Chicago but was permitted to continue pitching in Brooklyn. Not only that, but Seaman Grimes led the National League in pitching appearances, with forty.

Charles "Casey" Stengel, Dodgers right fielder and future Hall of Fame manager, was traded to the Pirates in 1918 and promptly enlisted in the navy. His military duties consisted of managing the Brooklyn Navy Yard's baseball team.

The baseball team at Boston's Charlestown Navy Yard, which came to be called the "Wild Waves," had a star-studded lineup of players from the Red Sox and the Braves, including Jack Barry, Ernie Shore, Del Gainer, Herb Pennock, Jim Cooney, Arthur Rico, and Henry Schreiber.

Giants pitcher Urban "Red" Faber, a future Hall of Fame member, spent his military time at the Great Lakes Naval Base, near Chicago. Yeoman Faber pitched for the Great Lakes baseball team until the armistice.

Duffy Lewis, Red Sox outfielder, spent the war at the Mare Island Naval Base near his hometown of San Francisco as player-manager of the baseball team.

Eddie Collins, who had been cheered when he came to the ballpark resplendent in his new marine uniform, spent his entire tour of duty at the Philadelphia Navy Yard. He was discharged with the Good Conduct Medal in time for spring training.

Al Schacht, baseball's future clown prince, was surprised when his hearing deficiencies did not keep him out of the draft. When he left the Bethlehem Steel League (BSL) in June, he played baseball stateside until his discharge.

EPILOGUE

A survey of available box scores for the 1918 season indicates that forty-five active and twenty-six retired Major Leaguers appeared in at least one game in the Bethlehem Steel League (BSL). The figures for the Delaware River Shipbuilding League (DRSL) are nine active and nine retired. In addition, scores of minor league players, active and retired, participated in both leagues.

Much public contempt was heaped upon the Major Leaguers, who were said to be playing in the "Safe Shelter Leagues." Sportswriters sometimes called them the "Paint and Putty" leagues, and when the Steel League began aggressively recruiting Major Leaguers, it became the "Steal League."

We can never know their motivations for taking jobs at the steel mills and shipyards, but a blanket label of "slacker" or the more modern "draft dodger" is inappropriate. However, we can say without reservation that there was a heavy measure of favoritism toward the ballplayers over the other workmen.

In the immediate wake of the Work-or-Fight Order, these "essential" jobs became highly prized because they came with draft exemptions. It was easy for farm boys, such as Phillies outfielder Frederick "Cy" Williams—they just went home. But most of the players, active and retired, chose steel or ships. Many other draft-age men also sought these jobs, but the ballplayers had the inside track because the industry magnates wanted a fast brand of baseball played at their plants. While ordinary men (those without great batting eyes or super fastballs) stood in line at the plants and shipyards and filled out employment applications, the ballplayers were recruited.

While many of the Major Leaguers were married and nominally draft-exempt, there was nevertheless great uncertainty and a feeling of vulnerability about one's draft status. This unease was due in large part to the fact that the Selective Service regulations, in the words of historian Gerald E. Shenk, "gave local and district boards 'exclusive jurisdiction' over the determination of exemptions and deferred classifications." In his book *"Work or Fight!" Race, Gender, and the Draft in World War One*, Shenk adds, "Local boards had considerable freedom to interpret and enforce the law as they saw fit."

To prove his point, we have to look no further than Babe Ruth and Joe Jackson. Ruth had registered with a Baltimore draft board in 1917 and received a deferment as a husband with a dependent wife. And while Ruth feigned unconcern about his draft status, when he contemplated leaving the Red Sox in his dispute with owner Harry Frazee, he wired the Chester team in the Shipyard League, asking to play there. On the other hand, not only did Jackson have a dependent wife; he was also supporting his mother and two younger siblings, and three of his brothers were already in uniform. Nevertheless, his Greenville, South Carolina, draft board rescinded his deferment and reclassified him as 1-A.

There was unfairness in the matter of money. The average pay in the mills, none of which was unionized, was about $1,500 a year. News reports of the time suggest that top Major Leaguers were paid $500 per game, lesser lights received $250 per game, and the minor leaguers slightly less. Money was a powerful tool in the hands of recruiters hired by the steel mills, and it was plentiful. For example, William G. Maurer, manager of the Lebanon team in the Steel League, sent this telegram to Major Leaguers: "Will you consider playing with us? If so wire us your lowest terms at our expense." One highly respected sportswriter, I. E. Sanborn of the *Chicago Tribune*, said that some players were offered $4,000 and $5,000 a year to play in the Steel League as well as in the Shipyard League. Some restrictions on players' remuneration were imposed by the government, but not until August.

Much effort by league officials went into painting a picture of the baseballers working regular plant shifts and then playing on weekends. This overalls-to-uniform image was almost certainly a fantasy for most. The intense rivalries between the mill teams and the mill owners suggest a more likely picture of everyday practices and limits on the work exertions of the ballplayers. In addition, many of the teams, including Lebanon and Bethlehem, played exhibition games during the week, which kept the players away from their essential work for at least the afternoon.

The National League claimed that an investigation of the Steelton and Lebanon clubs in the BSL showed that most of the Major League professionals "[we]re found at practice daily at their respective parks from two to four P.M. and d[id] not thereafter go back to work."

There is evidence that some players buckled down at their essential jobs and worked a full day. Chief Bender sometimes put in fourteen-hour days at Hog Island. His teammate, Hans Lobert, missed a game because he had to work. Jackson, who worked hard and spent his weekends raising money for the wartime effort, surely did more to defeat Germany than did the Major Leaguers who donned army uniforms to take up cushy stateside jobs as baseball managers and recreation directors.

But there was simmering resentment among the rank-and-file workers because of the special treatment accorded most of the players. Workers at Cramp's Shipyard in Philadelphia staged a one-day strike to protest players being paid more money for less work, with the freedom to "come and go as they please." Labor leaders at Hog Island complained that the players "had nothing to do except watch other men work" and "didn't know a bolt from a screw."

Historian Lindsay John Bell of University of Wisconsin-Eau Claire points out that the men who hired the ballplayers had a role in these Safe Shelter Leagues: "I think a greater emphasis on the complicity of people like Charles Schwab and others running the war industries mitigates the 'slacker' label lobbed at the ballplayers. The owners and managers of the shipyards and steel industries could have taken a hard stance by stating, 'Sorry, we aren't accepting the labor of ballplayers,' or if they did, at least prevent them from playing baseball. However, they saw an advantage of the conditions brought on by the war to profit off Major League players and they took it."

One thing is certain: The Steel and Shipyard Leagues were a good deal for the ballplayers and the men who hired them.

ACKNOWLEDGMENTS

I am deeply in debt to Denise Phillips, director of the Interlibrary Loan Department at the Hershey Public Library, who kept a steady stream of baseball books coming my way. I requested exactly 113 books. She delivered them all.

Jim Leeke has done extensive work on this period of baseball history, and I have leaned heavily on it. Anyone interested in this book will want to read his *From the Dugouts to the Trenches: Baseball during the Great War* and *The Best Team Over There: The Untold Story of Grover Cleveland Alexander and the Great War.*

My membership in the Society for American Baseball Research (SABR) placed a massive and indispensable trove of information at my fingertips.

I received guidance from historian Lindsay John Bell of University of Wisconsin-Eau Claire, whose specialty is the role of sports in early-twentieth-century U.S. history.

Three individuals read drafts of my book and made suggestions that resulted in measurable improvements. My son, Bill; my brother-in-law, Ken McClure; and my good friend and former *Philadelphia Inquirer* colleague, Art Carey.

I vacillated for several years over whether to write this book, and Ryan Mulligan, my editor at Temple University Press, badgered me at regular intervals to go ahead with it. He also solved a nagging difficulty in Chapter 5.

My wife, Susan, was another consistent advocate for this book, and it was she who finally convinced me to write it. Then, she persevered through the yearlong process of research and writing, reading drafts and making constructive suggestions.

APPENDIX

The summaries of individual games from the 1918 season are taken from stories in these newspapers: the *Allentown Democrat*, the *Allentown Morning Call*, *Harrisburg Telegraph*, *Harrisburg Courier*, the *Harrisburg Evening News*, *Lebanon Daily News*, *Lebanon Evening Report*, the *Lebanon Courier*, the *Philadelphia Inquirer*, the *Philadelphia Evening Telegraph*, *Philadelphia Public Ledger*, *Wilmington Evening Journal*, the *Wilmington Morning News*, the *Boston Globe*, *Camden Daily Courier*, and the *Baltimore Sun*.

Some of the descriptions here are also found in Chapter 5.

WEEKEND 1 [MAY 11–12]

Wilmington defeated Lebanon, 4–2, but Lebanon protested the game on the grounds that some Wilmington players violated eligibility rules. The protest was upheld by the league, which ordered that the game be replayed.

Both of the other Steel League opening games went into extra innings. Steelton defeated Bethlehem, 1–0, in ten innings. George Pierce (ex-Cardinals) and George "Buck" Ramsey, a fourteen-year minor leaguer, combined for the Steelton shutout. Sparrows Point traveled to Massachusetts and defeated Fore River in eleven innings by a score of 2–1. Catcher Aleck Smith (formerly of the Giants) drove in the winning run.

Each of the three first games of the season drew about 2,500 fans.

With far fewer Major Leaguers in uniform, the opening days in the Delaware River Shipbuilding League (DRSL) drew sparser crowds. Harlan defeated Merchant Ship, 4–1; Hog Island bested Merchant Ship, 8–0; Chester Ship took Sun Ship, 13–6; and New York Ship won, 5–0, over League Island Navy Yard, which would drop out of the Steel League after one more game and be replaced by Pusey & Jones.

WEEKEND 2 [MAY 18–19]

Some three thousand fans showed up in Steelton to watch Lebanon beat the home team, 4–3. Lebanon's Bill Ritter (formerly of the Giants) outpitched Steelton's Eddie Plank. Ritter ended the game by striking out third baseman Dick Neild with the bases loaded. Among the spectators was Branch Rickey, president of the St. Louis Cardinals, who came to meet with two Steelton players—Steve Yerkes, former second baseman for the Red Sox and the Cubs, and Bud Weiser, former Phillies outfielder—in an effort to recruit them to play for the Cardinals. His efforts were unsuccessful, and he left town empty-handed. As part of his struggle to fill the Cardinals roster with good players, Rickey had signed several Cuban ballplayers, who were draft-proof. Baseball had become popular in Cuba as part of the island nation's initiative to free itself from Spanish influence.

In other Steel League games, Fore River defeated Wilmington, 4–2. Al Mamaux, who had left the Dodgers several weeks earlier, was the winning pitcher over George Dumont. Joe Jackson still did not play. Meanwhile, Bethlehem bested Sparrows Point, 3–2, in ten innings. Bethlehem managed only three hits, but the Sparrows Point pitchers served up eight walks, and the winning run scored on a wild pitch. Al Schacht, the future "Clown Prince of Baseball," was the winning pitcher.

In Camden, New Jersey, New York Ship defeated Sun Ship, 2–1, before some two thousand fans. Chuck Moyer, New York shortstop, had a home run and two doubles. Harlan defeated Hog Island, 6–4, before some five thousand fans at Wilmington. Other games were not covered by newspapers.

WEEKEND 3 [MAY 25–26]

At Wilmington, the home team defeated Bethlehem, 3–2, as the visitors' third baseman, Ed Fitzpatrick (Braves), made four errors. The Sparrows Point at Steelton game was canceled because four of the visiting players were injured in a minor traffic accident. The Lebanon–Fore River game was rained out.

In the DRSL, Chester Ship beat Harlan, 4–3. Chester tied the score in the ninth inning and went on to win in the tenth. New York Ship edged Sun Ship, 2–1, and Merchants bested Traylor by an identical score.

DECORATION DAY

In Jackson's first game, Wilmington defeated Steelton, 2–1. The game was a pitcher's duel between two Major Leaguers, Steelton's Pierce (previously of the Chicago Cubs) and Harlan's Dumont (of the Washington Senators). Despite managing only two singles off Pierce, Harlan won in the ninth inning on an error by Steelton's first baseman. Steelton's left fielder, Herb Hunter (Chicago Cubs), had two hits in a losing cause.

The Shipyard League observed Decoration Day by playing exhibition games. In *From the Dugouts to the Trenches*, Jim Leeke says that the game between Chester Ship and Sun Ship illustrated that the DRSL was "a hard-scrabble shipyard league in wartime . . . and hardly a dreamy idyll. Several teams played their home games not in pastoral perfection, but within the confines of their own clanging shipyards."

The game story in the next day's *Chester Times* included this description: "On all four sides of the field are tents pitched for the shelter of a company of soldiers who are training and on guard duty at the plant. The sight was an attraction in itself and the boys went through their drills while the game was in progress. Another singular incident was the launching of a minesweeper by the Sun Company. The boat glided into the Delaware while the game was ending and no one knew anything of the launching."

WEEKEND 4 [JUNE 1–2]

Wilmington moved into first place by defeating Sparrows Point, 5–1. Jackson had two hits, but all of Wilmington's runs were unearned due to five Sparrows Point errors. Dumont limited the Maryland team to five hits. Sparrows Point received some good news after the game: Yankees outfielder Hugh High had taken a job at the shipyard and would be playing baseball. High was a good hitter, fielder, and base runner—all in short supply at Sparrows Point. In a game played on Schwab Field in Bethlehem, Lebanon won over the home team, 4–2, behind Ritter's two-hitter; Ritter struck out the side in the ninth inning to end the game. Lebanon's Norm Plitt (Dodgers) was hit by a pitch from Stan Baumgartner (Phillies) and would be out for two weeks. Steelton bested Fore River, 6–1, behind a strong performance from Plank. Fore River's Mamaux (Dodgers) was knocked out in the seventh inning. All three games drew large crowds.

Such was not the case in the Shipyard League, whose games drew sparse crowds and scant attention from newspaper sports pages. Harlan beat New York Ship, 4–3, in what the *Philadelphia Inquirer* described as a "slow and lifeless game." Merchants bested Pusey & Jones, 2–1, and Hog Island won over Sun Ship, 10–7. Chester Ship's victory over Traylor was not covered.

WEEKEND 5 [JUNE 8–9]

Wilmington consolidated its first-place lead in the standings in Week 5 with a convincing 4–0 win over Lebanon behind Dumont's five-hitter. Ritter was the losing pitcher. Jackson had two hits. Some three thousand fans witnessed the action at Lebanon's Cottage Hill Field. Bethlehem's Schacht shut out Steelton, 7–0, on three hits. George Twombly (Boston Braves) had a triple and cut off two Steelton runs with a shoestring catch. Fore River sent Sparrows Point to its fourth straight loss, 9–2. Clyde Engle (ex-Indians), John Dowd (ex-Yankees), and Larry Kopf (ex-Reds) each had two hits for the winners.

Some three thousand fans showed up in Camden, New Jersey, to watch the hometown New York Ship team hit three home runs to edge Pusey & Jones, 4–3. Harlan defeated Merchants, 5–1; Hog Island scored five runs in the first inning in its win over Traylor, 7–0; and Chester bested Sun Ship, 6–0.

WEEKEND 6 [JUNE 15–16]

Wilmington got a major boost in Week 6 when pitcher Lefty Williams and his batterymate Byrd Lynn infuriated Charles Comiskey by leaving the White Sox for jobs in the shipyard. Wilmington went on to defeat Fore River, 4–2; Dumont outpitched Mamaux (Dodgers). Engle (Cleveland Indians) had two hits, including a triple, for the losers. After the game, there was a concert by the Harlan band, followed by a minstrel show. Lest anyone read Lebanon's exhibition against the barnstorming Giants as a sign that the Steel League was immune to the culture of the time, minstrel shows featured entertainers in blackface who sang, danced, and performed comedy routines employing stereotypical versions of black Americans.

In other games, Steelton avenged an earlier loss by beating Lebanon, 3–1. Plank held the visitors to four hits. Jess Buckles (ex-Yankees) pitched well in his Steel League debut but had some control problems. Second baseman Yerkes (ex-Cubs) had a key hit for Steelton. Several hundred Lebanon fans made the trip by trolley to Steelton, which had just expanded its seating capacity to about three thousand. Sparrows Point edged Bethlehem, 1–0, as Ed Monroe (Yankees) pitched a six-hitter. Lefty Russell (Athletics) drove in the game's only run with a sharp single to left field. Second baseman Fitzpatrick (Braves) had two hits for Bethlehem.

In Shipyard League action, Chester Ship won its sixth consecutive game with a 2–0 victory over Pusey & Jones. Hog Island beat Harlan, 4–3, in extra innings. Sun Ship defeated Merchants, 7–2, and New York Ship won over Traylor, 3–1.

WEEKEND 7 [JUNE 22–23]

Bethlehem edged Wilmington, 1–0, behind the pitching of Jeff Tesreau, who had just left the New York Giants. Dumont shut out Bethlehem for eight innings, but second baseman Fitzpatrick (Braves) led off the ninth with a single, moved to second on a sacrifice by Paddy Baumann (Yankees), and scored the winning run on a single by Dave Wright, the catcher. Jackson had one of the seven hits off Tesreau. The game had to be stopped three times because of steady rain. Nevertheless, some 1,800 fans watched the entire game at Bethlehem.

Tesreau's arrival was fortuitous, as Bethlehem's pitcher Schacht had told the company that he had been drafted and left to serve in the army. According to the *Harrisburg Courier*, "The going of Schacht bears out the statement made by officials of the local club that no players would be lured to the local team on promises of industrial exemptions and that any within the draft age who did not rightfully earn an exemption by virtue of being an expert in the manufacture of munitions would have to report when called by the draft." When Schacht had come to Bethlehem in early May, he had told the company that he was classified as 1-A and expected to be called soon. The *Courier* said that Schacht would be missed: "During his stay here, Schacht became a great favorite with his teammates and was liked by all with whom he came into contact. Being always of a jocular nature . . . he entertained the boys with many humorous tales."

Dave Roth, a veteran minor leaguer and former Baltimore Oriole, led Sparrows Point to a 5–0 victory over Steelton. After the season, Roth would return to his home in Baltimore, where he would succumb to the Spanish flu in October. The Sparrows Point offense was led by Chick Fewster (Yankees), Runt Walsh (Phillies), and Lefty Russell (Athletics), who played first base even though he was listed on the roster as a pitcher. Hunter (Cubs) had two hits for the losers. Lebanon's game at Fore River was rained out.

In Shipyard League action, Chester Ship won its seventh straight game, handing Harlan a 3–0 loss with Twink Twining (ex-Reds) tossing a five-hitter before a crowd of five thousand. Chester scored all its runs in the third inning, when Harlan's Williams (White Sox) had trouble finding home plate, walking two and hitting another. Twining also managed two hits in his own at-bats.

In the days before the Chester-Harlan matchup, the *Philadelphia Public Ledger* speculated that the game would attract "the largest crowd that ever witnessed a game in Wilmington" and that it was "almost a certainty that Joe Jackson and other big leaguers w[ould] appear."

"I don't care who they play," snapped Chester manager Frank Miller. "We are going to win." Harlan manager Fred Gallagher said that if his club lost, he would "quit the league." Despite the loss, Harlan did stay in the league—wisely, as it turned out.

In other important games, New York Ship stayed close to Chester by beating Sun Ship, 3–2. Despite making three errors in the fourth inning that led to three unearned runs, Hog Island rallied to defeat Pusey & Jones, 6–4. Johnny Castle (ex-Phillies) had three hits and scored the winning run.

WEEKEND 8 [JUNE 29–30]

Sparrows Point bested Wilmington, 7–5, in what the *Wilmington Evening Journal* described as "one of the best games of the season in the Steel League," adding that "the infield work of both teams was sensational." Sparrows Point turned three double plays. Leading the Sparrows Point offense were three New York Yankees—John Priest, Chick Fewster, and Hugh High. Jackson had three hits, including a double, but in the fifth inning, he was ruled out for leaving the base path. As the July 1 deadline for the Work-or-Fight Order drew close, the exodus of American and National League players to the Steel League accelerated. The *Evening Journal* noted that the lineups of Sparrows Point and Wilmington consisted mostly of active and former Major Leaguers, which "pleased the 4000 fans."

Dutch Leonard (Giants) made his Steel League debut with Fore River but was outdueled by Steelton's Eddie Plank. In absorbing the 6–2 loss, Leonard had shoddy defensive support. Fore River committed five errors, including three by left fielder Olaf Henriksen (Red Sox). In Lebanon, two former New York Giants pitchers, Bethlehem's Tesreau and Lebanon's Ritter, clashed in a tight contest that was won by the home team, 4–2. Ritter gave up five hits, one of them a triple by right fielder Twombly (Braves). After the game, Ritter left to enlist in the U.S. Army. His spot in the Lebanon pitching rotation was filled by Alex Main (Phillies).

Over in the Shipyard League, Chester Ship stayed undefeated with a 5–2 win over Merchants. Hog Island won its fifth straight game and moved into second place with a 3–2 victory over New York Ship. Harlan scored five runs in the first inning and went on to trounce Traylor, 11–7. Lynn (White Sox) had two hits for the winners.

FOURTH OF JULY

The Steel League closed out the first half of its season in Week 8 with doubleheaders on the Fourth of July. Steelton defeated Wilmington twice. In the first game, Pierce (Cubs) scattered eight hits for a 4–1 victory. He held Jackson hitless until the eighth inning, when Shoeless Joe tripled. But he was stranded minutes later when Ed Gharrity (Senators) struck out. Dumont had control problems for the losers. In the afternoon game, Plank shut the visitors out, 2–0. Hunter (Cubs) led the Steelton offense with two hits. Jackson had one of Wilmington's four hits.

Lebanon and Sparrows Point also split their doubleheader. Sparrows Point won the opener, 4–3, behind the timely hitting of High (Yankees), who had three hits and drove in the winning run, and Russell (Athletics), who had two hits. Buckles (ex-Yankees) took the loss for Lebanon. Lebanon won the afternoon game, 5–2, behind Mains (Phillies), who made his Steel League debut. Second baseman Ambrose McConnell (ex–White Sox) had two hits for the winners.

Standings: Lebanon, 6–4; Steelton, 6–4; Wilmington, 5–5; Bethlehem, 4–6; Fore River, 3–7.

The Shipyard League teams played only exhibition games on the holiday.

WEEKEND 9 [JULY 6–7]

Jackson had a single and two walks to help Wilmington overcome first-place Lebanon, 9–4, and tighten the race for the Steel League pennant. Wilmington battered Main (Phillies) and Buckles (ex-Yankees) for nine hits, including a home run, three triples, and two doubles. Although on the roster as a pitcher, Joe Lake (ex-Tigers) made two sparkling defensive plays as a catcher for the winners. Tesreau (Giants) gave up nine hits to Steelton, but he was tough when it counted, and Bethlehem eked out a 4–3 win in eleven innings. The winning run crossed the plate after pitcher Pierce (ex-Cardinals) issued three walks and then made a throwing error. Steelton's Hunter (Cubs) drove in two runs with a triple in the sixth inning. Sparrows Point got seven hits off Leonard, including a home run and two triples, to defeat Fore River, 9–3.

Standings: Lebanon, 5–4; Wilmington, 6–5; Steelton, 6–5; Sparrows Point, 6–5; Bethlehem, 6–6; Fore River, 3–7.

In the Shipyard League, New York Ship handed Chester its first loss of the season, 7–5, at Camden, New Jersey. Chester pitcher Twining (Reds) was knocked out in the fifth inning by a three-run homer. At Bristol, Pennsylvania, Hog Island bested Merchants, 6–3, behind a strong performance by Chief Bender, who also had three hits. The victory moved Hog Island to within a half-game of league-leading Chester. Sun Ship won its third consecutive game by besting Harlan, 5–1.

Standings: Chester Ship, 8–1; Hog Island, 7–1; New York Ship, 7–2; Harlan, 5–4; Merchants, 3–5; Sun Ship, 3–7; Pusey & Jones, 0–7; Trayor, 0–6.

WEEKEND 10 [JULY 13–14]

Steelton knocked Lebanon out of first place before three thousand spectators. Steelton's Plank held the home team to seven hits. Main (Phillies) again pitched poorly. He was hit in the head by a line drive off Plank's bat and had to leave the game; he was relieved by Buckles (ex-Yankees). Yerkes (ex-Cubs) had three hits, including a triple, and Hunter (Cubs) drove in two runs with a triple.

Bethlehem's Tesreau pitched a two-hitter to defeat Sparrows Point, 5–2. The Marylanders had a golden opportunity in the first inning when they loaded the bases on two errors and a walk. But Tesreau struck out High (Yankees) to end the threat. Pitcher Roth, formerly with the Baltimore Orioles of the International League, suffered his first loss after four consecutive wins. Earl Blackburn (ex-Cubs), George Twombly (Braves), and Paddy Baumann (ex-Yankees) led the Bethlehem offense. High robbed Tesreau of a home run with a leaping catch. Second baseman Fewster (Yankees) stifled a Bethlehem rally in the fourth inning with a spectacular catch.

In Quincy, Massachusetts, Fore River's Leonard limited Wilmington to five hits and struck out eight in a 7–0 victory. Fore River scored five runs in the first inning to knock out Wilmington's Dumont. Ken Nash (ex-Indians) led the Fore River offense with two hits. A few days earlier, Nash had been named a district judge by Governor Samuel W. McCall. John Dowd (ex-Yankees), Clyde Engle (Indians), Merwin Jacobson (ex-Cubs), Larry Kopf (ex-Reds), and Tom Daly (ex–White Sox) also wielded big bats in Fore River's victory.

In Shipyard League action, Harlan reached a low point in the season by losing 2–0 to previously winless Pusey & Jones. Harlan had only three hits, two of them by Lynn (White Sox). P&J fans threw a raucous celebration in the shipyard following the game. In another upset, Merchant Ship bested New York Ship, 9–0, with the help of six errors by the losers.

Standings: Chester, 9–1; Hog Island, 7–2; New York Ship, 7–3; Harlan, 5–5; Merchant Ship, 4–5; Sun Ship, 3–7; Pusey & Jones, 1–7; Traylor, 0–6.

WEEKEND 11 [JULY 20–21]

Two former big leaguers pitched shutouts, and Steelton won a doubleheader at Sparrows Point. In the first game, Plank won his sixth straight decision, shutting out the visitors on four hits. Allen Russell (Senators) made his Steel League debut for Sparrows Point and was battered for fourteen hits. Roxey Roach (ex-Senators) and Bud Weiser (ex-Phillies) had multiple hit games for Steelton, and Plank helped himself by driving in one of the runs. Steelton second baseman Yerkes (ex-Cubs) injured his leg while making a sensational catch to rob High (Yankees) of an extra base hit and had to be carried off the field. It was expected that he would not return during the season. In the second game, Pierce (ex-Cardinals) also held the Marylanders to four hits and won by a score of 3–0. Jack Stutz, who replaced Yerkes at second base, paced the winners with two hits.

At Lebanon, Fore River's Leonard shut out the home team, 4–0. Ritter returned from his military duties in Pittsburgh for one last game but was rusty and ineffective. Right fielder Joe Connolly (Braves), catcher Tom Daly (ex-Reds), and second baseman John Dowd (ex-Yankees) all had two hits for Fore River. The *Lebanon Daily News* alleged that Ritter's loss "was not entirely his fault." Its headline read, "UMPIRE REILLY SCORED FOR HIS RANK DECISIONS. HIS INCOMPETENCY AS AN ARBITER APPARENT." The article elaborated:

> The incompetence of umpire Reilly was never more apparent than in the critical stages of the game. He missed a clear attempt on the part of Dowd to bunt [with two strikes] and a chance was thereby lost to hold Fore River's score to two runs. This same Reilly called Babbington out in the second inning on a play at third base when the local left fielder was clearly safe and broke up a drive on Leonard which promised much for the locals. Reilly's work, never anywhere near league caliber, was even worse than his previous performances in this city.

For the first time in the 1918 season, Pop Kelchner, who had scouted so many of the team's stars, took over as Lebanon's manager, and his appearance in uniform drew an ovation from the hometown fans.

The umpiring also came into question at Wilmington, where the home team won, 2–1, over Bethlehem. Dumont pitched a two-hitter and drove in the winning run with a controversial triple. A record crowd of 4,500 was on hand, and those who could not find seats encircled the field, sitting on the grass. The crowd was not roped off from the playing field. This circumstance, according to the *Allentown Democrat*, was "responsible for near-riots on several occasions." The paper said that the work of the umpires, particularly the plate umpire, "was erratic and almost resulted in calling the game off." With Wilmington leading 1–0 in the third inning, Bethlehem third baseman Baumann (ex-Yankees) singled and scored on a triple to deep center field by second baseman Fitzpatrick (Braves). But the umpire ruled that the ball rolled into the crowd, limited Fitzpatrick to a double, and ordered Baumann back to third. The inning ended without Bethlehem scoring. Bethlehem filed a protest, but it was denied. In the seventh inning, with the score tied 1–1, Dumont apparently drove in the winning run with a triple to deep center field, but the umpire initially ruled that the ball went into the crowd, and Dumont was limited to a ground-rule double—as Fitzpatrick had been in the third inning. However, at this point, Jackson raced onto the field, pointed to a spot on it, and said that was where the ball had landed. The umpire agreed and ordered Dumont to third base and the runner home with the go-ahead run. Several Bethlehem players threatened the umpire physically, and he had to be protected by two policemen. The next day's *Wilmington News* praised Jackson's "quick thinking and great knowledge of the game." Catcher Lake (ex-Tigers) had two hits for the winners. Tesreau took the loss for Wilmington.

Standings: Steelton, 9–5; Wilmington, 7–6; Bethlehem, 7–7; Lebanon, 5–6; Sparrows Point, 6–8; Fore River, 5–7.

In Shipyard League play, Harlan made a significant change that would be expanded in the weeks to come; three players from the Wilmington Steel League team were moved over to play for the Harlan Shipyard League nine, which went on to beat Pusey & Jones, 5–2, with Lefty Williams (White Sox) pitching a five-hitter. George Mangus (ex-Phillies) had two hits for Harlan, and Lynn (White Sox) was Williams's batterymate. Some 3,500 spectators showed up for this match.

Chester Ship improved its record to 10–1 with a 15–7 win over Merchant Ship. Forrest Cady (Athletics) and Jim Eschen (ex-Indians) had multiple hits for Chester. Under the headline "Chester Gets Pennant," the *Philadelphia Public Ledger* wrote, "Frank Miller and his crowd of Chester clouters have captured the championship of the Delaware River Ship League. They visited Bristol on Saturday and had a slugfest at the expense of Merchants." But the pennant award was premature.

Standings: Chester, 10–1; New York Ship, 8–3; Hog Island, 7–3; Harlan, 6–5; Merchants, 4–6; Sun Ship, 4–7; Pusey & Jones, 1–8; Traylor 0–7.

WEEKEND 12 [JULY 27–28]

Pitching dominated Week 11 of the Steel League, as all six hurlers were active or retired Major Leaguers. Steelton's Plank and Fore River's Leonard baffled opposing hitters for the entire game. Leonard struck out eleven. Steelton scored the game's only run in the eighth inning on a walk, an error by third baseman Connolly (Braves), and an infield hit. Plank gave up only three hits, two of them by first baseman Engle (ex-Indians). Steelton's Roach (ex-Senators) made several standout defensive plays from shortstop. When he left the field in the ninth inning, Leonard received an ovation from many of the three thousand attending Steelton fans. The *Harrisburg Telegraph* noted that the umpire, Augie Moran, "had an off day," adding, "The Philadelphian made numerous bad decisions and was criticized on many occasions by the players. Moran has been here quite a few times this season, and up to this time made a big hit with the fans." As Steelton won, the poor decisions were soon forgotten.

On July 27, Plank of Steelton ceded only three hits on his way to defeating

Leonard (who only gave up four hits), 1–0. Leonard walked in the only run of the game in the eighth inning. Bethlehem bested Lebanon in another 1–0 game: a pitchers' duel between Bethlehem's Tesreau and Lebanon's Buckles (ex-Yankees). The lone run was scored in the eighth inning when Sam Fishburn, the future St. Louis Cardinal, reached first base on an error, stole second, reached third on an error, and scored on a sacrifice fly by Fitzpatrick (Braves). Walter Holke (Giants), making his debut at first base for Bethlehem, went hitless but was applauded several times by the crowd of four thousand when he figured in defensive plays.

Dumont allowed only four hits as Wilmington defeated Sparrows Point, 3–1, at the losers' field. Allen Russell (Senators) pitched well for Sparrows Point, but several errors were costly. Third baseman Gus Getz (Pirates) had two hits for Wilmington, and Jackson played center field and had a single.

Standings: Steelton, 10–5; Wilmington, 7–6; Bethlehem, 8–7; Sparrows Point, 6–8; Lebanon, 5–7; Fore River, 5–8.

In the Shipyard League, the weekend ended with a three-way tie for first place. Harlan easily defeated Sun Ship, 9–0. Williams (White Sox) pitched the two-hit shutout and was opposed on the mound by a Sun Ship pitcher who played for the Swarthmore College team. Williams also had a double and a home run. Once again, three Steel League players suited up to play for Harlan. Hog Island stayed in the running for the pennant by beating Merchants Ship, 13–6. Bender pitched for Hog Island but was ineffective and had to be replaced in the fourth inning. The game was played on Hog Island's new athletic field, built at a cost of $90,000 (about $1.7 million in 2022). Traylor ended its winless drought by taking two games from Pusey & Jones, notably with the help of pitcher Chick Holmes, an Athletics rookie who had just left Philadelphia to work at Traylor. Indeed, Holmes pitched both games, winning the first, 3–0, and the second, 2–1. He gave up a total of only eight hits over eighteen innings. The Chester–New York Ship game was rained out.

Standings: Chester, 9–2; New York Ship, 9–2; Hog Island, 9–2; Harlan, 8–2; Merchants, 3–8; Traylor, 2–7; Sun Ship, 2–9.

WEEKEND 13 [AUGUST 3–4]

Week 12 in the Steel League saw Bethlehem stun Steelton, 6–0, behind the pitching of Tesreau. He was opposed by Plank, who gave up thirteen hits in his poorest performance of the season. Plank had won seven straight Steel League games. The *Harrisburg Telegraph* speculated that "Eddie had just received word that his peach crop . . . near Gettysburg would be a failure and instead of throwing a horsehide he thought he was handling a succulent peach." Despite the loss, two newcomers to the Steelton club, left fielder Johnny Beall (Cardinals) and second baseman Joe McCarthy, the future Hall of Fame manager, played well. Catcher Blackburn (ex-Cubs) and second baseman Fitzpatrick (Braves) had extra base hits for the winners. Bethlehem moved to within one game of the league leaders.

Lebanon's Buckles (ex-Yankees) held Wilmington to four hits, one of them by Jackson, in a 3–2 victory at home. Dumont pitched well, but lapses by the Wilmington defenders were costly. Wilmington lost despite having seven Major Leaguers in its starting lineup—a testament to the level of competition in the Steel League.

Sparrows Point traveled to Fore River and handed the home team a 5–3 loss. Leonard gave up only four hits, but he was hurt by four errors, including two by shortstop Kopf (ex-Reds). Pitcher Lefty Russell (Athletics) played first base and had three hits for Sparrows Point; second baseman Fewster (Yankees) had two hits. Fore River batters were led by right fielder Connolly, who had three hits, including a triple.

Standings: Steelton, 10–6; Bethlehem, 9–7; Wilmington, 7–7; Sparrows Point, 7–8; Lebanon, 6–7; Fore River, 5–9.

With Hog Island missing its only two Major Leaguers, Chester Ship won by a score of 9–6. Bender had suffered a skull fracture and a broken wrist in a work accident, and infielder Hans Lobert (ex-Giants) had to miss the game to prepare for the launching of a ship. Hog Island showed up with only eight players, but Chester lent them an outfielder. Chester scored five runs in the second inning, mostly due to sloppy Hog Island fielding. New York Ship defeated Merchants Ship to stay tied for the league lead with Chester. At the last minute, Traylor informed Harlan that it would have to forfeit the game because five of its players had enlisted in the army. Some two thousand Harlan fans waited for about an hour before being informed that their team had been awarded a 9–0 forfeit.

Standings (top teams only): Chester, 10–2; New York Ship, 10–2; Hog Island, 9–3; Harlan, 9–4.

WEEKEND 14 [AUGUST 10–11]

Steelton solidified its grip on first place in Week 13 with a 6–3 win over Lebanon. Losing with a score of 3–1, Steelton scored five runs in the seventh inning to take the lead, chasing starting pitcher Buckles (ex-Yankees) to the showers. The *Lebanon Evening Report* said that the cheers from the three thousand hometown fans were so loud, they could be heard on the other side of the mile-wide Susquehanna River. Right fielder Herb Hunter (Cubs) and third baseman Jack Knight (future Cardinals) each had two hits for the winners. Third baseman Mike Mowrey (Dodgers) had a home run for Lebanon.

Wilmington edged Fore River, 7–5, as Jackson drove in the winning runs in the eighth inning with a two-run double. Only one of Fore River's runs was earned, as Wilmington made four errors; pitcher Mamaux (Dodgers) came in with the bases loaded and no outs in the seventh inning and struck out the next three batters. Only about one thousand spectators were on hand for the action. The next day, Mamaux was in Woonsocket, Rhode Island, pitching for the Fisk Red Tops in the New England Semi-professional Championship. Mamaux pitched nine strong innings and had two hits, including a double. The Red Tops beat Queen Quality, 8–3. Another Steel Leaguer on the Fore River roster, Dowd (ex-Yankees), played shortstop for the winners.

Sparrows Point broke up a scoreless game in the ninth inning for a 3–0 victory over Bethlehem. The Marylanders scored all their runs off Tesreau. Second baseman Fewster (Yankees) had two hits for Sparrows Point.

Standings: Steelton, 11–6; Wilmington, 9–7; Bethlehem, 9–8; Sparrows Point, 8–9; Lebanon, 6–8; Fore Rover, 5–10.

In the Shipyard League, Harlan moved seven Major Leaguers over from the Wilmington Steel League team and easily whipped the league-leading New York Ship, 10–0. In contrast to the meager attendance at the Wilmington game on Saturday, some 3,500 fans watched the action. New York brought only eleven players, only one of whom, Wid Conroy (ex-Yankees), had Major League experience. Catcher Lake (ex-Tigers) and second baseman Getz (Pirates) each had three hits for Harlan. Jackson was in Reading, playing a benefit game, as he usually did on Sundays.

The game from first pitch to final out took only one hour and twenty-seven minutes. Most of the Steel League and Shipyard League games were completed in two hours or less, which was in line with the American and National Leagues at the time. Today, average Major League games run about three hours. Fans blame pitchers taking too much time between offerings, too long breaks between innings, replay reviews, and frequent pitching changes for the long games.

In other Shipyard League contests, Hog Island defeated Sun Ship, 7–2. Lobert (ex-Giants) made his debut for Hog Island at second base. Bender did not play, still recovering from his work injuries. Chester Ship stayed in first place with an easy 9–0 win over Traylor.

Standings at the top of the league: Chester Ship, 11–2; Hog Island, 11–3; New York Ship, 11–3; Harlan, 9–4.

WEEKEND 15 [AUGUST 17–18]

Week 14 in the Steel League saw the pennant race tighten as Sparrows Point bested first-place Steelton, 4–3, while second-place Bethlehem beat Wilmington, 2–1.

Steelton could have clinched the title, but Plank gave up eleven hits in a poor outing. Fewster (Yankees) had three hits, including a double and triple, and also made several outstanding defensive plays at second base for Sparrows Point. Walsh (ex-Phillies) had two hits, including a double, for the winners. Steelton's offense was led by second baseman McCarthy. Sparrows Point pitcher Roth, formerly with the Baltimore Orioles, had won three straight pitcher's duels against Plank, Tesreau, and Leonard.

Bethlehem moved within one game of Steelton in a contest against Wilmington that was marred by near riots. Bethlehem's Tesreau held the visitors to four hits, including two by Jackson. Fishburn, the future St. Louis Cardinal, had four hits for Bethlehem. The game was held up in the fourth inning for about five minutes when the Wilmington team disputed the decision of the umpire, calling right fielder Gharrity (Senators) out on strikes. Gharrity's teammate Lake (ex-Tigers) became enraged and struck the umpire in the back of the neck, knocking him to the ground. "This nearly caused a riot," the *Baltimore Sun* reported, "but the field was cleared and the game resumed." The *Allentown Democrat* opined, "The unsportsmanlike conduct of the Wilmington catcher was resented by the crowd and only the promptness of the police prevented a riot."

Lebanon and Fore River split a doubleheader in Massachusetts.

Standings: Steelton, 11–7; Bethlehem, 10–8; Wilmington, 9–8; Sparrows Point, 9–9; Lebanon, 7–9; Fore River, 7–11.

In the Shipyard League, New York Ship upset Chester Ship, 2–0. Chester managed only two hits, and two Major Leaguers—Eschen (ex-Indians) and Cady (Athletics)—were held hitless. According to the *Chester Times*, "The game was witnessed by one of the biggest crowds of the season. Special cars carried more than a thousand shipbuilders to the game besides other fans."

Harlan played its second stringers and almost lost, edging a weak Pusey & Jones team to stay in the running for the pennant.

WEEKEND 16 [AUGUST 24–25]

Wilmington defeated Sparrows Point.

Steelton failed in another attempt to secure the pennant by losing to last-place Fore River, 5–0, behind Dutch Leonard. Some four thousand fans watched approvingly. Plank had another off-day for the Pennsylvanians. Bethlehem moved into a first-place tie with Steelton by defeating Lebanon, 2–1. Bethlehem scored both runs in the fourth inning when right fielder Twombly (Braves) and third baseman Baumann (Yankees) singled and then moved to second and third on a ground out. Twombly scored on an error, and Baumann scored the decisive run on a single by catcher Blackburn (ex-Cubs).

Bethlehem kept pace with Steelton by knocking off Fore River, 6–1. Tesreau gave up ten hits, but he spaced them well and was never in serious trouble. Bethlehem nicked Fore River's Mamaux (Dodgers) for eleven hits, including three doubles and a triple. Twombly (Braves) and Baumann (Yankees) each had three hits for Bethlehem.

WEEKEND 17 [AUGUST 31–SEPTEMBER 1]

The Steel League was to close out its season with the possibility of a three-way tie for first place as Wilmington prepared to take on Steelton.

However, Steelton put an end to that possibility three days later by climactically defeating Wilmington, 3–2, in eleven innings. Lefty Williams pitched well for Wilmington, striking out fourteen batters, but he had trouble with third baseman Jack Knight (ex-Yankees). In the first inning, Jackson crashed into the center field wall while chasing down a triple by Knight. With the score tied 2–2 in the eleventh, McCarthy lifted a fly ball to right field that dropped for a triple when Joe Jackson and Ed Gharrity (Senators) collided. McCarthy raced to third base, and Knight singled him home for the decisive tally. His two collisions clearly weighing on him, Jackson limped off the field as the game ended. The latter collision may have owed to Gharrity playing catcher, not outfielder, over his career with the Senators. Bethlehem defeated Lebanon, and the regular Bethlehem Steel League (BSL) season ended with Steelton and Bethlehem tied for the pennant.

Final standings: Steelton, 11–8; Bethlehem, 11–8; Wilmington, 10–9; Sparrows Point, 9–10; Lebanon, 8–10; Fore River, 7–11.

NOTES

Abbreviations

CT—*Chicago Tribune*
NYS—*New York Sun*
NYT—*New York Times*
NYTR—*New York Tribune*
PI—*Philadelphia Inquirer*
PPL—*Philadelphia Public Ledger*
SABR—Society for American Baseball Research
SLST—*St. Louis Star and Times*
WEJ—*Wilmington Evening Journal*
WMN—*Wilmington Morning News*

Prologue

In the early fall of 1918: Babe Ruth's batting habits and techniques are a composite taken from Thomas Barthel, *Babe Ruth and the Creation of the Celebrity Athlete* (Jefferson, NC: McFarland, 2018); Robert Creamer, *Babe: The Legend Comes to Life* (New York: Simon and Schuster, 1974); Bill Jenkinson, *The Year Babe Ruth Hit 104 Home Runs* (Cambridge, MA: Da Capo, 2007); Glenn Stoudt, *The Selling of the Babe* (New York: Thomas Dunne Books, 2016); and Kal Wagenheim, *Babe Ruth: His Life and Legend* (New York: Open Road, 2014).

Then, George Herman "Babe" Ruth connected: Ed Rose, "Pop Kelchner, Gentleman Jake, the Giant-Killer, and the Kane Mountaineers," *Baseball Research Journal* 40, no. 1 (Spring 2012).

The next day, in Reading: Rogers Hornsby's batting habits and techniques are a composite taken from Charles C. Alexander, *Ty Cobb* (New York: Oxford University Press, 1985); Jonathan D'Amore, *Rogers Hornsby: A Biography (Baseball's All-Time Greatest Hitters)* (Westport, CT: Greenwood, 2004); and C. Paul Rogers III, "Rogers Hornsby," SABR, https://sabr.org/bioproj/person/rogers-hornsby/.

The pitcher released the ball: *WEJ*, September 11, 1918.

Around the same time of year: Joe Jackson's batting habits and techniques are a composite taken from David L. Fleitz, *Shoeless: The Life and Times of Joe Jackson* (Jefferson, NC: McFarland, 2001); Kelly Boyer Sagert, *Joe Jackson: A Biography* (Westport, CT: Greenwood, 2004); and David Fleitz, "Shoeless Joe Jackson," SABR, https://sabr.org/bioproj/person/shoeless-joe-jackson/.

Shoeless Joe Jackson easily connected: "The Delaware River Shipbuilding League," *The National Pastime*, 2013, 13.

Rogers Hornsby . . . a .358 lifetime average: Rogers, "Rogers Hornsby," SABR.

Joe Jackson . . . the third highest in history: Fleitz, "Shoeless Joe Jackson," SABR.

Chapter 1

One and a half years earlier: "Yankees Fall Before Red Sox," *NYT*, April 12, 1917; "Yankees Better Soldiers Than Baseball Players," *NYTR*, April 12, 1917; "Yankees March," *NYS*, April 1, 1917.

The *New York Times* reported: "Yankees Fall Before Red Sox," *NYT*, April 12, 1917.

About this same time: "Cravath's Vicious Drives Saved Alex," *PI*, April 12, 1917.

At Shibe Park in Philadelphia: "Johnson's Speed Blinded Macks," *PI*, April 12, 1917.

An hour later, in St. Louis: "Many Fans Disappointed Over Failure to See Browns and Sox Maneuver," *SLST*, April 12, 1917.

The following week, in Chicago: "27,000 See Sox Drop Opening to Braves," *CT*, April 20, 1917.

While the forces: Charles C. Alexander, *Ty Cobb* (New York: Oxford University Press, 1985), 130.

Huston's idea was quickly: "Huston's Plan Is Favored," *City Journal*, Sioux City, IA, February 27, 1917.

The Yankees held their spring training: Jim Leeke, *From the Dugouts to the Trenches: Baseball during the Great War* (Lincoln: University of Nebraska Press, 2017), 3.

Meanwhile, out in Mineral Wells: "Baseball Bats Used as Rifles in White Sox Camp," *Sacramento Star*, March 24, 1917.

There were army drill instructors: Leeke, *From the Dugouts to the Trenches*, 12–13.

The opening of the 1917 Major League Baseball: Martin Gilbert, *A History of the Twentieth Century*, vol. 1 (New York: William Morrow, 1999), 437–438.

General John J. Pershing, commander: Leigh Montville, *The Big Bam: The Life and Times of Babe Ruth* (New York: Doubleday, 2006), 62.

Wilson expected one million: David L. Fleitz, *Shoeless: The Life and Times of Joe Jackson* (Jefferson, NC: McFarland, 2001), 147–148.

The implementation of the draft: "Conscription, World War I," Encylopedia.com, https://www.encyclopedia.com/defense/energy-government-and-defense-magazines/conscription-world-war-I.

National League president John Tener: Paul Hensler, "'Patriotic Industry': Baseball's Reluctant Sacrifice in World War I," The Free Library, March 22, 2013, https://tinyurl.com/2p9cdwm6.

According to his biographer Leigh Montville: Montville, *The Big Bam*, 62.

On July 20, 1917: Leeke, *From the Dugouts to the Trenches*, 41–42.

According to historian Patricia O'Toole: Patricia O'Toole, "How the US Government Used Propaganda to Sell Americans on World War I," History.com, March 28, 2023, https://www.history.com/news/world-war-1-propaganda-woodrow-wilson-fake-news.

Few words were more defamatory: David Kluft, "When 'Slacker' Was a Dirty Word: Defamation and Draft Dodging during World War I," Trademark and Copyright Law, June 30, 2014, https://www.trademarkandcopyrightlawblog.com/2014/06/when-slacker-was-a-dirty-word-defamation-and-draft-dodging-during-world-war-i/.

"Nothing further than a uniform": Leeke, *From the Dugouts to the Trenches*, 28–29.

Clark Griffith, owner: Robert Elias, *The Empire Strikes Out* (New York: New Press, 2010), 79.

General Pershing, commander: Elias, *The Empire Strikes Out*, 79.

When actor Douglas Fairbanks: Elias, *The Empire Strikes Out*, 79.

There was a White Sox "patriotic button": "Old Fighter Designs Patriotic Sox Button," *CT*, October 16, 1917.

When the White Sox showed up: Hensler, "'Patriotic Industry.'"

Huston, who was an army colonel: "Baseball's Bit in the War," *Baseball Magazine*, March 1918.

In addition to manpower: Winthrop Smith, *Catching Lightning in a Bottle: How Merrill Lynch Revolutionized the Financial World* (New York: Wiley, 2013), 71–74.

MLB players and teams took part: Elias, *The Empire Strikes Out*, 80.

In his 2010 book: Elias, *The Empire Strikes Out*, 77.

The National League's Tener opined: Elias, *The Empire Strikes Out*, 79.

Charles Murphy, a former Chicago Cubs owner: Elias, *The Empire Strikes Out*, 84.

According to *American Boy* magazine: Elias, *The Empire Strikes Out*, 86.

At the sprawling Great Lakes Naval Station: Elias, *The Empire Strikes Out*, 86.

Yankees owner Huston: Elias, *The Empire Strikes Out*, 87.

The War Department's Commission on Training Camp Activities: Elias, *The Empire Strikes Out*, 88.

***Stars and Stripes*, the daily:** Elias, *The Empire Strikes Out*, 88.

Recruitment posters pictured: Elias, *The Empire Strikes Out*, 87.

Sportswriter William Heyliger: Elias, *The Empire Strikes Out*, 87.

***Baseball Magazine* blamed:** Elias, *The Empire Strikes Out*, 90.

General Pershing claimed: Elias, *The Empire Strikes Out*, 87.

Indeed, as the 1917 season opened: "The Baseball Grenade," *Whitewright Sun*, Whitewright, TX, April 17, 1917.

Several months later: "Baseball Players Make Poor Grenade Hurlers," *Washington Times*, July 30, 1917.

They had already used: Elias, *The Empire Strikes Out*, 86.

"Enthusiasm is a fine thing": Hensler, "'Patriotic Industry.'"

Reach Athletic Goods: Elias, *The Empire Strikes Out*, 79.

Harry Von Tilzer: Elias, *The Empire Strikes Out*, 80.

Even before the war declaration: "Raising National Patriotism and Recruitment," The United States World War One Centennial Commission, https://www.worldwar1centennial.org/index.php/the-politics-and-propaganda-of-tin-pan-alley/raising-national-patriotism-and-recruitment.html.

The movie industry sought: "Over Here: WWI and the Fight for the American Mind," New York Public Library, https://www.nypl.org/events/exhibitions/overhere/more.

Johnson went to Washington: Elias, *The Empire Strikes Out*, 82.

In an effort to bolster Johnson's plan: "Donation of Game's Profits to Uncle Sam Rickey's Idea," *Tulsa Democrat*, December 5, 1917.

The $500 was to be distributed: "Baseball Men Awake," *Washington Times*, March 24, 1918.

It would be another seven seasons: "Tune In on W-G-N," *CT*, April 14, 1925.

Chapter 2

"Charlie excelled not only as a singer": Robert Hessen, *Steel Titan* (Pittsburgh: University of Pittsburgh Press, 1975), 10.

When Schwab was twelve: Hessen, *Steel Titan*, 6.

Here, he went to a high school: William S. Dietrich II, "Smilin' Charlie Schwab: Life on a Large Canvas," *Pittsburgh Quarterly*, Spring 2010, https://pittsburghquarterly.com/articles/smilin-charlie-schwab/.

One of Schwab's teachers: Hessen, *Steel Titan*, 10.

In his personal life: Hessen, *Steel Titan*, 18.

Schwab declined because of a disagreement: Hessen, *Steel Titan*, 62.

After Jones was killed: Dietrich, "Smilin' Charlie Schwab."

A reporter for the *New York Sun*: Dietrich, "Smilin' Charlie Schwab."

But the profits of Bethlehem Steel: Dietrich, "Smilin' Charlie Schwab."

He was accused, unfairly, of fraud: Dietrich, "Smilin' Charlie Schwab."

Charlie and Rana held: Daniel Alef, *Charles M. Schwab: King of Bethlehem Steel* (Santa Barbara, CA: Titans of Fortune Publishing, 2009), Kindle edition, location 29.

In fact, when Carnegie lay on his deathbed: Dietrich, "Smilin' Charlie Schwab."

The 12,000-ton order: "Beam Let the Steel Reach New Heights," *The Morning Call*, March 4, 2007, https://www.mcall.com/news/mc-xpm-2007-03-04-3712893-story.html.

Schwab had gambled: Amy Lamare, "The Story of a 19th Century Steel Tycoon Who Squandered His $800 Million Fortune and Died Broke," Celebrity Net Worth, September 10, 2015, https://www.celebritynetworth.com/articles/entertainment-articles/american-steel-magnate-charles-m-schwab-blew-fortune-worth-500-800-million-dollars/.

In testimony before Congress: Dietrich, "Smilin' Charlie Schwab."

The British countered with: Alef, *Charles M. Schwab*, Kindle edition, location 74.

"To the last resources": "Beam Let the Steel Reach New Heights."

Early in his days at Bethlehem Steel: Hessen, *Steel Titan*, 185.

In a brief, fawning history: Arundel Cotter, *The Story of Bethlehem Steel* (New York: Moody Magazine and Book Company, 1910), 21.

Some soccer historians say: Clemente Lisi, "Soccer History: Bethlehem Steel," United States National Soccer Team Players Association, July 30, 2018, https://ussoccerplayers.com/2018/07/soccer-history-bethlehem-steel.html.

"Chas. M. Schwab has become a base hall [*sic*] magnate": "Munition Workers Will Have Baseball League," *Allentown Democrat*, February 12, 1916.

Schwab gave these instructions: "When the Sultan of Swat Played for the Men of Steel," ArcelorMittal USA, August 31, 2017, https://usa.arcelormittal.com/news-and-media/our-stories/2017/aug/08-31-2017.

Way, a Yale graduate: "Way Holds Fore River to 4 Hits in Steel League Game," *Boston Globe*, June 10, 1917.

The *Lebanon Evening Report* complained: "Neutral Umpiring Needed," *Lebanon Evening Report*, August 13, 1917.

The next day, the *Lebanon Evening Report* gushed: "Lebanon Champions in Bethlehem Steel League," *Lebanon Evening Report*, September 4, 1917.

Historian Dietrich notes: Dietrich, "Smilin' Charlie Schwab."

The combination of unchecked spending: Lamare, "The Story of a 19th Century Steel Tycoon Who Squandered His $800 Million Fortune and Died Broke."

Chapter 3

The tone was set at the White House: John L. Barry, *The Great Influenza* (New York: Penguin Group, 2004), 96.

Everybody but the men managing baseball: Jim Leeke, *From the Dugouts to the Trenches: Baseball during the Great War* (Lincoln: University of Nebraska Press, 2017), 76–79.

Only Charles Ebbets: Leeke, *From the Dugouts to the Trenches*, 78.

But Huston found allies: "'Baseball Men, Awake,' Is Yank Moguls Word from Army in France," *Washington Times*, March 24, 1918.

The *New York Tribune* advised: "Random Thoughts," *NYTR*, March 25, 1918.

Night games under lights: Norm King, "May 24, 1935: Reds Fans See the Lights in First Night Game in MLB History," SABR, 2019, https://sabr.org/gamesproj/game/may-24-1935-reds-fans-see-the-lights-in-first-night-game-in-mlb-history/.

Nevertheless, some of the owners reasoned: "Baseball Slacker If Games Open Late, Wasting Daylight," *Anaconda Standard*, Anaconda, MT, April 28, 1918.

Charles L. Pack: "Opposed to Plan of Later Games," *NYT*, April 2, 1918.

"The professional baseball league": "Baseball Slacker If Games Open Late."

The Duluth team: Leeke, *From the Dugouts to the Trenches*, 114; "Sports of All Sorts," *Troy Times*, May 15, 1918.

***Baseball Magazine* reported:** "Say It Wasn't So: Joe Jackson, World War I's Most Famous Baseball Slacker," Doug Wilson Baseball, February 2017, http://dougwilsonbaseball.blogspot.com/2017/02/say-it-wasnt-so-joe-jackson-world-war.html?m=1 (accessed February 21, 2022).

Throughout his career, Plank: Jan Finkel, "Eddie Plank," SABR, https://sabr.org/bioproj/person/eddie-plank/.

During one of these early games: Harvey Frommer, *Shoeless Joe and Ragtime Baseball* (New York: Lyons Press, 2016), 27.

"The oddest character": "Say It Wasn't So."

According to Donald Gropman: Donald Gropman, *Say It Ain't So, Joe!* (Boston: Little, Brown, 1979), 147–148.

Perhaps it was a mistake: David L. Fleitz, *Shoeless: The Life and Times of Joe Jackson* (Jefferson, NC: McFarland, 2001), 149.

After talking to Jackson by telephone: Fleitz, *Shoeless*, 151.

The *Chicago Tribune* published: Gropman, *Say It Ain't So, Joe!*, 148.

A *Tribune* columnist: Gropman, *Say It Ain't So, Joe!*, 149.

Ban Johnson leaped: Leeke, *From the Dugouts to the Trenches*, 94.

White Sox owner Charles Comiskey hinted: Leeke, *From the Dugouts to the Trenches*, 95.

The *Chicago Tribune* noted: Gropman, *Say It Ain't So, Joe!*, 153.

The defections of Williams and Byrd: Robert Elias, *The Empire Strikes Out: How Baseball Sold U.S. Foreign Policy and Promoted the American Way Abroad* (New York: New Press, 2010), 84.

***The Sporting News* was a dependable advocate:** "Say It Wasn't So."

In *From the Dugouts to the Trenches*, Jim Leeke says, "All": Leeke, *From the Dugouts to the Trenches*, 95.

"It makes no difference": Fleitz, *Shoeless*, 152.

"I can't understand why Jackson": "Say It Wasn't So."

Another defender was: Gropman, *Say It Ain't So, Joe!*, 149.

A week after he arrived in Wilmington: Gropman, *Say It Ain't So, Joe!*, 150.

In an article published in *Delaware History*: Peter T. Dalleo and J. Vincent Watchorn III, "Slugger or Slacker? Shoeless Joe Jackson and Baseball in Wilmington, 1918," *Delaware History* (Fall–Winter 1994–1995), 104.

Kelly Boyer Sagert, a Jackson biographer: Kelly Boyer Sagert, *Joe Jackson: A Biography* (Westport, CT: Greenwood, 2004), 75.

Jackson biographer David L. Fleitz: Fleitz, *Shoeless*, 150.

One Georgia board: David M. Kennedy, *Over Here: The First World War and American Society* (New York: Oxford University Press, 2004), 156.

Governor Martin Brumbaugh of Pennsylvania: Kennedy, *Over Here*, 156.

"Baseball is a secondary consideration": Tom Swift, *Chief Bender's Burden* (Lincoln: University of Nebraska Press, 2008), 122.

Connie Mack, who managed him: Robert Peyton Wiggins, *Chief Bender* (Jefferson, NC: McFarland, 2010), 47.

. . . with racist "war whoops.": Curt Brown, "White Earth to World Series: Charles Bender's Bittersweet Baseball Story," *Minneapolis Star-Tribune*, August 8, 2020.

During his playing years: Brown, "White Earth to World Series."

When he died the following year: Brown, "White Earth to World Series."

"There is a limit to how long": Swift, *Chief Bender's Burden*, 145.

Crowder explained that the order: Dalleo and Watchorn, "Slugger or Slacker?," 105.

Among the nonessential pursuits: Elias, *The Empire Strikes Out*, 72.

"If I had my way": Ty Waterman and Mel Springer, *The Year the Red Sox Won the Series* (Boston: Northeastern University Press, 1999), 83.

Red Sox owner Harry Frazee insisted: Waterman and Springer, *The Year the Red Sox Won the Series*, 84.

Barney Dreyfuss: Paul Hensler, "'Patriotic Industry': Baseball's Reluctant Sacrifice in World War I," The Free Library, March 22, 2013, https://tinyurl.com/2p9cdwm6.

Some journalists gloated: Dalleo and Watchorn, "Slugger or Slacker?"

The next day, a *St. Louis Post-Dispatch* reporter wrote: Tim O'Neil, "A Look Back: Worker Struggles, Racial Hatred in East St. Louis Explodes in White Rioting," *St. Louis Post-Dispatch*, July 1, 2012.

The *Washington Times* said: "Steel League Agents Raid Major Leagues," *Washington Times*, June 20, 1918.

And the *Pittsburgh Press* noted: "Steel League to Pay Some Large Salaries," *Pittsburgh Press*, April 25, 1918.

Tesreau, a burly farm boy: Leeke, *From the Dugouts to the Trenches*, 92.

"I know of my own personal knowledge": Untitled, *Chicago Times*, June 3, 1918.

"If the Government needs": Christy Mathewson, *Managing in a Moment: Baseball Observations (1916 to 1918) Leading Up to and during the Great War* (Newhall, CA: Mathewson Foundation, 2018), Kindle edition, location 204.

"The war that had rearranged borders": Leigh Montville, *The Big Bam: The Life and Times of Babe Ruth* (New York: Doubleday, 2006), 80.

"Silver nitrate could be effective": Evan Bleier, "Remembering the Pandemic That Nearly Killed Babe Ruth," InsideHook, April 2, 2020, https://www.insidehook.com/article/sports/influenza-pandemic-that-nearly-killed-babe-ruth.

When Barrow suggested that Ruth: Robert Creamer, *Babe: The Legend Comes to Life* (New York: Simon and Schuster, 1974), 162.

When the slugger returned to the dugout: Creamer, *Babe*, 162.

The next day, the *Chester Times*: Creamer, *Babe*, 163.

When a reporter asked Frazee: Creamer, *Babe*, 163.

"No, that's not it at all": Creamer, *Babe*, 163.

Grantland Rice: Randy Roberts and Johnny Smith, *War Fever* (New York: Basic Books, 2020), 180.

The armed forces newspapers: Roberts and Smith, *War Fever*, 180.
Then, *Stars and Stripes* dropped the sports page: Roberts and Smith, *War Fever*, 180.
The boilerplate affidavits: Hensler, "'Patriotic Industry.'"
But a few days later: Hensler, "'Patriotic Industry.'"
"Baseball Will Lose": Waterman and Springer, *The Year the Red Sox Won the Series*, 143.
Red Sox owner Frazee: Roberts and Smith, *War Fever*, 178.
They defended "the national pastime": Roberts and Smith, *War Fever*, 178.
Hugh S. Fullerton wrote: Leeke, *From the Dugouts to the Trenches*, 79.
A popular song appeared: Waterman and Springer, *The Year the Red Sox Won the Series*, 162.
He had told the draft board: Murray Polnar, *Branch Rickey* (Jefferson, NC: McFarland, 2007), 75.
The *Pittsburgh Press* noted, "Rog": "Hornsby in Class Three," *Pittsburgh Press*, January 26, 1918.
Rickey's biographer Lee Lowenfish: Lee Lowenfish, *Branch Rickey: Baseball's Ferocious Gentleman* (Lincoln: University of Nebraska Press, 2007), 147.

Chapter 4

"It's our game, America's game": "Baseball: America's Game, Art and Objects from the Bank of America Collection," Haggin Museum, https://hagginmuseum.org/exhibitions/baseball-americas-game-art-and-objects-from-the-bank-of-america-collection/.
"Every section of the country": Jim Leeke, *From the Dugouts to the Trenches: Baseball during the Great War* (Lincoln: University of Nebraska Press, 2017), 90.
Baseball historian Heather S. Shores: Heather S. Shores, "Working to Play, Playing to Work: The Northwest Georgia Textile League," *The National Pastime*, 2010, 44.
A biographer, Ted Schwarz: Ted Schwarz, *Joseph P. Kennedy: The Mogul, the Mob, the Statesman, and the Making of an American Myth* (Hoboken, NJ: Wiley, 2003), 79.
Kennedy believed that: David Nasaw, *The Patriarch: The Remarkable Life and Turbulent Times of Joseph P. Kennedy* (New York: Penguin Press, 2012), 55–56.
Leonard pitched for Fore River: Schwarz, *Joseph P. Kennedy*, 55.
According to *Maryland Historical Magazine*: "Slugger or Slacker?" *Maryland Historical Magazine* 98, no. 1 (Spring 1998), 111.

Chapter 5 (and Appendix)

One game in July: Brian McKenna, "Bethlehem Steel League," SABR, https://sabr.org/bioproj/topic/bethlehem-steel-league/.

That same afternoon: "Boston Red Sox Attendance Data," Baseball Almanac, https://www.baseball-almanac.com/teams/rsoxatte.shtml.

The *Wilmington Evening News* noted: Peter T. Dalleo and J. Vincent Watchorn III, "Slugger or Slacker? Shoeless Joe Jackson and Baseball in Wilmington, 1918," *Delaware History* (Fall–Winter 1994–1995), 113.

One publicity blurb read: Dalleo and Watchorn, "Slugger or Slacker?," 113.

Although the origin of the term: "Doughboys," National World War I Museum and Memorial, https://www.theworldwar.org/learn/about-wwi/doughboys.

The *Philadelphia Inquirer* reported: "Harlan Wins in Eighth Inning," *PI*, May 31, 1918.

The *Wilmington Morning News* said: "Harlan Wins over Steelton, Score 2–1," *WMN*, May 31, 1918.

The next morning: "Harlan Wins over Steelton, Score 2–1."

. . . although at one point: "When Babe Ruth Played for Lebanon More Than 100 Years Ago," *LebTown*, September 15, 2018.

John B. Sheridan: "Battle of Belleau Wood Begins," History.com, February 9, 2010, https://www.history.com/this-day-in-history/battle-of-belleau-wood-begins.

The citation read: "Battle of Belleau Wood Begins."

"Men crammed together": G. J. Meyer, *The World Remade: America in World War I* (New York: Random House, 2016), 406.

He singled and then stole second base: "Harlan Teams Win and Lose Games," *WEJ*, June 17, 1918.

The *Philadelphia Public Ledger* opined: "Kauff May Star on Shipyard Team," *PPL*, June 27, 1918.

Yankees business manager Harry Sparrow: Jim Leeke, *From the Dugouts to the Trenches: Baseball during the Great War* (Lincoln: University of Nebraska Press, 2017), 93.

The *New York Sun* reported: Leeke, *From the Dugouts to the Trenches*, 93.

The *Washington Times* offered: "Ban Johnson Will Ask Protection from Steel League Blandishments," *Washington Times*, June 19, 1918.

According to Georgia Tech history professor: Melissa August, "This Year's World Series Isn't the First Played during a Pandemic. Here's What Happened to Baseball in 1918," *TIME*, October 23, 2020, https://time.com/5903122/pandemic-world-series/.

"The story of Babe Ruth's mighty hitting": Randy Roberts and Johnny Smith, "When Babe Ruth and the Great Influenza Gripped Boston,"

Smithsonian, April 30, 2020, https://www.smithsonianmag.com/history/when-babe-ruth-and-great-influenza-gripped-boston-180974776/.

Leon Cadore, a pitcher with the Brooklyn Dodgers: Robert Elias, *The Empire Strikes Out: How Baseball Sold U.S. Foreign Policy and Promoted the American Way Abroad* (New York: New Press, 2010), 89.

***Baseball Magazine* ran:** Elias, *The Empire Strikes Out*, 89.

The *Boston Transcript* tortured: Elias, *The Empire Strikes Out*, 89.

Editorials like this one: Meyer, *The World Remade*, 332.

"During the last two years of the war": Randy Roberts and Johnny Smith, *War Fever* (New York: Basic Books, 2020), 14.

"Joe could have used the letter": Donald Gropman, *Say It Ain't So, Joe!* (Boston: Little, Brown, 1979), 151–152.

In the days before the Chester-Harlan matchup: "Big Game at Doylestown Will Be Chief Feature," *PPL*, June 15, 1918.

Harlan manager Fred Gallagher: Jim Leeke, "The Delaware River Shipbuilding League, 1918," SABR, https://sabr.org/journal/article/the-delaware-river-shipbuilding-league-1918/.

"For when a man built a mill or factory": Frederick Lewis Allen, *The Big Change* (New York: Harper, 1952), 49.

On Week 7, the last weekend in June: "Brown's Triple Defeats Harlands," *WEJ*, July 1, 1918.

The *Washington Times* reported: "National Game Should Gain Added Life and Spirit in Suspension," *Washington Times*, July 21, 1918.

This circumstance, according to the *Allentown Democrat*: "Shoddy Umpiring in Bethlehem Loss to Wilmington," *Allentown Democrat*, July 22, 1918.

The next day's *Wilmington News*: "Both Harlan Teams Come Through in Biggest Baseball Bill in Years," *WMN*, July 22, 1918.

As *Baseball Magazine* put it: "Scott Perry and the Number Three," *Baseball Magazine*, October 1918.

"I found a *New York Herald* paper": Daniel Wrinn, *World War One: WWI History Told from the Trenches, Seas, Skies, and Desert of a War Torn World* (New York: Storyteller Books, 2021), Kindle edition, 144.

The next day, the *Wilmington Morning News*: Dalleo and Watchorn, "Slugger or Slacker?," 94.

The most common argument: Dalleo and Watchorn, "Slugger or Slacker?," 89.

On August 5, the *Harrisburg Evening News*: "Trench Proof," *Harrisburg Evening News*, August 5, 1918.

As far away as Utah: "Memory of Fan Probably Will Take the Edge off of Interest in Men Who Seek Good Bombproof Jobs under the Work or Fight Order," *Ogden Standard*, August 10, 1918.

***The Sporting News* carried a satirical poem:** Elias, *The Empire Strikes Out*, 84.

And *The Sporting News* offered this further bit of sarcasm: Leeke, *From the Dugouts to the Trenches*, 98.

Beneath the headline: Ty Waterman and Mel Springer, *The Year the Red Sox Won the Series* (Boston: Northeastern University Press, 1999), 187.

Frank Bancroft: Leeke, *From the Dugouts to the Trenches*, 93.

"I will never join": "Sports Stars Turned Doughboys 'Over There,'" *VFW Magazine*, October 2013, 23.

"We are making no effort": "Hog Island Not Recruiting Major Leaguers," *News-Journal*, Mansfield, OH, August 5, 1918.

On August 14, Charles Schwab's subordinate: "No Favors to Players," *NYT*, August 15, 1918.

The *Allentown Democrat* opined: "Steel Team Defeats Wilmington and Tightens Steel League Race," *Allentown Democrat*, August 19, 1918.

The *Chester Times* complained: Leeke, "The Delaware River Shipbuilding League."

The move prompted *Philadelphia Inquirer* sportswriter Edgar Wolfe: Leeke, "The Delaware River Shipbuilding League."

The *Harrisburg Telegraph* said that Jackson's: "Steelton Tied with Bethlehem," *Harrisburg Telegraph*, September 2, 1918.

That total is deceptive: "1918: All Work or Fight and No Play," *This Great Game*, https://thisgreatgame.com/1918-baseball-history/.

"The Indians preferred to take a chance": Paul Hensler, "'Patriotic Industry': Baseball's Reluctant Sacrifice in World War I," The Free Library, March 22, 2013, https://tinyurl.com/2p9cdwm6.

Chapter 6

The *Harrisburg Telegraph* proclaimed: "World Series Baseball Here," *Harrisburg Telegraph*, September 5, 1918.

The *Wilmington Evening Journal* carried this lede: "Harlan Makes It Two Straight Wins," *WEJ*, September 9, 1918.

"It was all he could do to reach": "Harlan Winner of Second Game," *PI*, September 9, 1918.

"Harlan looked like a beaten team": "Jackson's Homers Defeat Standards," *NYS*, September 15, 1918.

The *New York Times* covered the game: "Harlan Nine in Triumph," *NYT*, September 9, 1918.

The *Philadelphia Inquirer* gave this description: "Harlan Team of Wilmington Wins Championship of Shipyard League," *PI*, September 15, 1918.

In a slap at the hometown Phillies: "Harlan Team of Wilmington Wins Championship of Shipyard League."

The *Inquirer* said that the second blast: "Harlan Team of Wilmington Wins Championship of Shipyard League."

The *Evening Public Ledger* covered: "Harlan Wins Cox Trophy," *Evening Public Ledger*, September 15, 1918.

"Some day Frazee will learn": Ty Waterman and Mel Springer, *The Year the Red Sox Won the Series* (Boston: Northeastern University Press, 1999), 195.

"Ban Johnson, in a less-than-sober state": "1918: All Work or Fight and No Play," *This Great Game*, https://thisgreatgame.com/1918-baseball-history/.

The *New York Times* captured the moment: "Red Sox Beat Cubs in Initial Battle of World's Series," *NYT*, September 6, 1918.

"With five weeks": Untitled, *Baseball Magazine*, December 1918.

But sportswriter Joe S. Jackson: "Work or Fight Order No Bar to Barnstorming Down East," *Detroit News*, September 26, 1918.

Two days later, Ruth accepted a job: Allen Wood, *Babe Ruth and the 1918 Red Sox* (Bloomington, IN: iUniverse Star, 2000), 121.

The next day's *Harrisburg Telegraph* was headlined: "Good Night! Lebanon Gets Babe Ruth," *Harrisburg Telegraph*, September 26, 1918.

The *Harrisburg Patriot* said that the area was lucky: "Ruth Coming to Lebanon," *Harrisburg Patriot*, September 27, 1918.

The *Baltimore Sun* was pleased: "Ruth May Come Here," *Baltimore Sun*, September 28, 1918.

Noting that the regular Steel League season was over: "Lebanon Fortunate in Securing Babe Ruth," *Lebanon Daily News*, September 28, 1918.

That night, the *Lebanon Evening Report* predicted: "Babe Ruth to Be in Uniform in Game Sat.," *Lebanon Evening Report*, September 27, 1918.

In addition, Kelchner recalled: Ed Rose, "Pop Kelchner, Gentleman Jake, the Giant-Killer, and the Kane Mountaineers," *Baseball Research Journal* 40, no. 1 (Spring 2012), available at https://sabr.org/journal/article/pop-kelchner-gentleman-jake-the-giant-killer-and-the-kane-mountaineers/.

While writing an article on the BSL: "When Babe Ruth Was No Hero," *Philadelphia Inquirer Magazine*, April 1, 1987, 15.

The *Lebanon Daily News* speculated that Ruth: "Last Game of Season on the Morrow," *Lebanon Daily News*, October 4, 1918.

The *Baltimore Sun* headlined: "Spanish 'Flu' Knocks Out Babe Ruth," *Baltimore Sun*, October 6, 1918.

Ruth had bought the farm: Kal Wagenheim, *Babe Ruth: His Life and Legend* (New York: Open Road, 2014), 89.

Ironically, though, when Japanese soldiers: "When Babe Ruth Was No Hero."

The *Lebanon News* lamented: "When Babe Ruth Was No Hero," 16.

"And both met a number of the local baseball followers": "Hornsby Spending Part of Honeymoon in Reading," *Reading Times*, October 7, 1918.

The day after the one-sided game: "Stronger Teams for Rest of Season at Lauer's Park," *Reading Times*, September 17, 1918.

They also said that the ballplayers "c[ame] and [went] as they please[d]": "Ball Players Cost Strike," *Wilkes-Barre Record*, September 21, 1918.

Whenever a journalist asked a striker: "Driver Slackers from Ship Yards," *Gettysburg Times*, September 21, 1918.

The *New York Tribune* tossed a log on that fire: "U.S. to Act to Oust Ship Work Slackers," *NYTR*, September 23, 1918.

They singled out such players as Pep Young: "Looking 'em Over," *Washington Times*, September 21, 1918.

Under the headline, "Hornsby": "Hornsby to Make Home in Reading," *Reading Times*, October 10, 1918.

The *Reading Eagle* said: "Hornsby Moving Belongings Here," *Reading Eagle*, October 10, 1918.

That same day, the *Lebanon Daily News*: "$100,000 Star Short Stop for Lebanon Team," *Lebanon Daily News*, October 10, 1918.

E. W. Dickerson, president of the Central League: "Wants Slackers Barred from Baseball," *PI*, February 1, 1919.

From Kentucky, the *Paducah Sun-Democrat*: "No Baseball for Slackers," *Paducah Sun-Democrat*, February 3, 1919.

The *El Paso Herald* added: "Local Citizens Very Patriotic," *El Paso Herald*, February 11, 1919.

White Sox owner Charles Comiskey: Donald Gropman, *Say It Ain't So, Joe!* (Boston: Little, Brown, 1979), 149.

On March 15, 1919: Untitled, *NYT*, March 15, 1919.

Chapter 7

"I saw Christy Mathewson doomed to die": Richard Gurtowski, "Remembering Baseball Hall of Famers Who Served in the Chemical Corps," The Free Library, July 1, 2005, https://www.thefreelibrary.com/emembering+baseball+hall+of+famers+who+served+in+the+Chemical+Corps.-a0137875685.

The official manual for the unit: Charles Leerhsen, *Ty Cobb: A Terrible Beauty* (New York: Simon and Schuster, 2015), 137.

Cobb explained why he had chosen: Al Stump, *Cobb: A Biography* (Chapel Hill, NC: Algonquin Books, 1994), 275.

Cobb's patriotic manifestations inspired: Ty Waterman and Mel Springer,

The Year the Red Sox Won the Series (Boston: Northeastern University Press, 1999), 162.

Cobb described what happened: Stump, *Cobb*, 276.

"Ty, I got a good dose": Stump, *Cobb*, 276.

"No one will have a chance": "Sports Stars Turned Doughboys 'Over There,'" *VFW Magazine*, October 2013, 23.

Baseball historian Jan Finkel suggests: Jan Finkel, "Pete Alexander," SABR, https://sabr.org/bioproj/person/pete-alexander/.

"Alcohol was taking over his life": Finkel, "Pete Alexander."

Finkel writes that Alexander's retirement years: Finkel, "Pete Alexander."

Jim Leeke writes: Jim Leeke, *The Best Team Over There: The Untold Story of Grover Cleveland Alexander and the Great War* (Lincoln: University of Nebraska Press, 2021), Kindle edition, 1.

Rickey, who led the front office: Finkel, "Pete Alexander."

In a letter to a friend: Leeke, *The Best Team Over There*, 136.

And he wrote this: Leeke, *The Best Team Over There*, 136.

And Lambeth, who had been born in Berlin, Kansas: Leeke, *The Best Team Over There*, 135.

In a letter to Dodgers owner: Leeke, *The Best Team Over There*, 94.

In another letter to Ebbets: Leeke, *The Best Team Over There*, 165.

His hometown newspaper: Leeke, *The Best Team Over There*, 184.

(It was said that due to his Ivy League pedigree): Kevin Coyne, "When Major Leaguer Eddie Grant Made the Ultimate Sacrifice," *Smithsonian*, October 2004, https://www.smithsonianmag.com/history/eddie-grant-baseball-player-world-war-i-180728112/.

When the United States entered the war in 1917, Grant: Coyne, "When Major Leaguer Eddie Grant Made the Ultimate Sacrifice."

Jay lifted his head: Tom Simon, "Eddie Grant," SABR, https://sabr.org/bioproj/person/eddie-grant/.

Leeke estimates that sixty active: Jim Leeke, *From the Dugouts to the Trenches: Baseball during the Great War* (Lincoln: University of Nebraska Press, 2017), 189.

He told *The Sporting News*: Joseph Wancho, "Gabby Street," SABR, https://sabr.org/bioproj/person/gabby-street/.

Cadore was unstinting in his praise: Warren Corbett, "Leon Cadore," SABR, https://sabr.org/bioproj/person/leon-cadore/.

Today's average nine-inning game: Wynn Montgomery, "That Was Quick!" SABR, https://sabr.org/journal/article/that-was-quick/.

"We have been scrapping": Jacob Pomrenke, "Joe Jenkins," SABR, https://sabr.org/bioproj/person/joe-jenkins/.

More than forty years later: Pomrenke, "Joe Jenkins."

He captured two German soldiers single-handedly: Jim Leeke, "Hughie Miller," SABR, https://sabr.org/bioproj/person/hughie-miller/.

Several newspapers reported that Huston: Leeke, "Hughie Miller."

In December 1918, *Baseball Magazine*: "Closing Events of the 1918 Baseball Season," *Baseball Magazine*, December 1918.

Epilogue

This unease was due in large part: Gerald E. Shenk, *"Work or Fight!" Race, Gender, and the Draft in World War One* (New York: Palgrave MacMillan, 2005), 168.

For example, William G. Maurer: Letter, June 20, 1918, from John A. Heydler, secretary-treasurer of the National League, to J. H. Ward, Bethlehem Steel Corp.

One highly respected sportswriter: David L. Fleitz, *Shoeless: The Life and Times of Joe Jackson* (Jefferson, NC: McFarland, 2001), 150.

The National League claimed that: Letter from John A. Heydler.

Workers at Cramp's Shipyard: "When Babe Ruth Was No Hero," *Philadelphia Inquirer Magazine*, April 1, 1987.

Historian Lindsay John Bell: Interview with John Lindsay Bell, November 16, 2022.

SELECTED BIBLIOGRAPHY

Abrahamson, James L. *The American Home Front*. Colorado Springs: Patrick Henry University Press, 2001.

Adie, Kate. *Fighting on the Home Front*. London: Hodder and Stoughton, 2013.

Akin, William E. *The Middle Atlantic League*. Jefferson, NC: McFarland, 2015.

Alef, Daniel. *Charles M. Schwab: King of Bethlehem Steel*. Santa Barbara, CA: Titans of Fortune Publishing, 2009.

Alexander, Charles C. *Rogers Hornsby: A Biography*. New York: Holt, 1995.

———. *Ty Cobb*. New York: Oxford University Press, 1984.

Allen, Frederick Lewis. *The Big Change*. New York: Harper, 1952.

Barnes, Alexander F., Peter L. Belmonte, and Samuel O. Barnes. *Play Ball! Doughboys and Baseball during the Great War*. Atglen, PA: Schiffer Publishing, 2019.

Barnette, Curtis. *Bethlehem Steel Corporation*. New York: Newcomen Society, 1995.

Barry, John L. *The Great Influenza*. New York: Penguin Group, 2004.

Barthel, Thomas. *Babe Ruth and the Creation of the Celebrity Athlete*. Jefferson, NC: McFarland, 2018.

———. *Baseball Barnstorming and Exhibition Games*. Jefferson, NC: McFarland, 2007.

Breen, William J. *Uncle Sam at Home: Civilian Mobilization, Wartime Federalism, and the Council of National Defense, 1917–1919*. Westport, CT: Greenwood Press, 1984.

Cobb, Ty. *My Life in Baseball*. Garden City, NY: Doubleday, 1961.

Cooksley, Peter G. *The Home Front*. Gloucestershire: Tempus Publishing, 2006.

Cotter, Arundel. *The Story of Bethlehem Steel*. New York: Moody Magazine and Book Company, 1916.

Creamer, Robert. *Babe: The Legend Comes to Life*. New York: Simon and Schuster, 1974.

D'Amore, Jonathan. *Rogers Hornsby: A Biography (Baseball's All-Time Greatest Hitters)*. Westport, CT: Greenwood, 2004.

Durso, Joseph. *Baseball and the American Dream*. Charlotte, NC: Sporting News, 1986.

Elias, Robert. *The Empire Strikes Out: How Baseball Sold U.S. Foreign Policy and Promoted the American Way Abroad*. New York: New Press, 2010.

Fischer, Claude S., and Michael Hout. *Century of Difference: How America Changed in the Last One Hundred Years*. New York: Russell Sage Foundation, 2006.

Fleitz, David L. *Shoeless: The Life and Times of Joe Jackson*. Jefferson, NC: McFarland, 2001.

Frommer, Harvey. *Shoeless Joe and Ragtime Baseball*. New York: Lyons Press, 2016.

Gaines, Bob. *Christy Mathewson, the Christian Gentleman*. Lanham, MD: Rowman and Littlefield, 2015.

Gilbert, Martin. *A History of the Twentieth Century*. Vol. 1. New York: William Morrow, 1999.

Giordano, Ralph. *Fun and Games in Twentieth-Century America*. Westport, CT: Greenwood Press, 2003.

Green, Harvey. *The Uncertainty of Everyday Life, 1915–1945*. Fayetteville: University of Arkansas Press, 2000.

Gropman, Donald. *Say It Ain't So, Joe!* Boston: Little, Brown, 1979.

Halfon, Mark S. *Tales from the Deadball Era*. Sterling, VA: Potomac Books, 2014.

Harper, Arthur. *How You Played the Game*. Columbia: University of Missouri Press, 1999.

Harries, Meirion, and Susie Harries. *The Last Days of Innocence, America at War, 1917–1918*. New York: Random House, 1997.

Heaphy, Leslie A. *The Negro Leagues, 1868–1960*. Jefferson, NC: McFarland, 2003.

Heidler, David S., and Jeanne T. Heidler. *Daily Lives of Civilians in Wartime Modern America*. Westport, CT: Greenwood Press, 2007.

Hessen, Robert. *Steel Titan*. Pittsburgh: University of Pittsburgh Press, 1975.

Hogan, Lawrence. *Shades of Glory*. Washington, DC: National Geographic, 2006.

Hornsby, Rogers. *My War with Baseball*. New York: Coward-McCann, 1962.

Huhn, Rick. *The Sizzler: George Sisler, Baseball's Forgotten Great*. Columbia:

University of Missouri Press, 2004.

Jenkinson, Bill. *The Year Babe Ruth Hit 104 Home Runs.* Cambridge, MA: Da Capo Press, 2007.

Kennedy, David M. *Over Here: The First World War and American Society.* New York: Oxford University Press, 2004.

Koppett, Leonard. *Concise History of Major League Baseball.* New York: Carroll and Graf, 2004.

Lee, Bill "Spaceman," and Jim Prime. *The Little Red Sox Book.* Chicago: Triumph Books, 2003.

Leeke, Jim. *The Best Team Over There: The Untold Story of Grover Cleveland Alexander and the Great War.* Lincoln: University of Nebraska Press, 2021. Kindle edition.

———. *From the Dugouts to the Trenches: Baseball during the Great War.* Lincoln: University of Nebraska Press, 2017.

Leerhsen, Charles. *Ty Cobb: A Terrible Beauty.* New York: Simon and Schuster, 2015.

Lengel, Edward G. *Never in Finer Company.* Lebanon, IN: Da Capo Press, 2018.

Levy, Alan H. *Joe McCarthy: Architect of the Yankee Dynasty.* Jefferson, NC: McFarland, 2005.

Lowenfish, Lee. *Branch Rickey: Baseball's Ferocious Gentleman.* Lincoln: University of Nebraska Press, 2007.

Macht, Norman. *Connie Mack and the Early Years of Baseball.* Lincoln: University of Nebraska Press, 2007.

Manley, Effa, and Leo Herbert Hardwick. *Negro Baseball . . . before Integration.* Haworth, NJ: St. Johann Press, 1976.

Mathewson, Christy. *Managing in a Moment: Baseball Observations (1916 to 1918) Leading Up to and during the Great War.* Newhall, CA: Mathewson Foundation, 2018. Kindle edition.

McGerr, Michael. *A Fierce Discontent: The Rise and Fall of the Progressive Movement in America, 1870–1920.* New York: Oxford University Press, 2005.

McKissack, Patricia C., and Fredrick McKissack. *Black Diamond: The Story of the Negro Baseball Leagues.* New York: Scholastic, 1994.

Mead, Gary. *The Doughboys: America and the First World War.* London: Lume Books, 2015.

Meyer, G. J. *The World Remade: America in World War I.* New York: Random House, 2016.

Montville, Leigh. *The Big Bam: The Life and Times of Babe Ruth.* New York: Doubleday, 2006.

Nasaw, David. *The Patriarch: The Remarkable Life and Turbulent Times of Joseph P. Kennedy.* New York: Penguin Press, 2012.

Polnar, Murray. *Branch Rickey.* Jefferson, NC: McFarland, 2007.

Prenau, David. *Seize the Daylight.* New York: Thunder's Mount Press, 2005.

Pustz, Matthew. *Baseball Follows the Flag.* Edmonton: University of Alberta, 1990.

Riley, James A. *The Biographical Encyclopedia of the Negro Baseball Leagues.* New York: Carroll and Graf, 1994.

Roberts, Randy, and Johnny Smith. *War Fever.* New York: Basic Books, 2020.

Robowsky, Mark. *A Complete History of the Negro Leagues.* New York: Birch Lane Press, 1995.

Rogosin, Don. *Invisible Men: Life in Baseball's Negro Leagues.* Lincoln: University of Nebraska Press, 1983.

Sagert, Kelly Boyer. *Joe Jackson: A Biography.* Westport, CT: Greenwood, 2004.

Schwarz, Ted. *Joseph P. Kennedy: The Mogul, the Mob, the Statesman, and the Making of an American Myth.* Hoboken, NJ: Wiley, 2003.

Seib, Philip. *The Player: Christy Mathewson, Baseball, and the American Century.* New York: Four Walls Eight Windows, 2003.

Seymour, Harold. *Baseball: The People's Game.* New York: Oxford University Press, 1990.

Shenk, Gerald E. *"Work or Fight!" Race, Gender, and the Draft in World War One.* New York: Palgrave MacMillan, 2005.

Skipper, John C. *Wicked Curve: The Life and Troubled Times of Grover Cleveland Alexander.* Jefferson, NC: McFarland, 2006.

Smiley, Anthony. *The Homefront.* London: BiblioScholar, 2012.

Smith, Winthrop. *Catching Lightning in a Bottle: How Merrill Lynch Revolutionized the Financial World.* New York: Wiley, 2013.

Spinney, Laura. *Pale Rider: The Spanish Flu of 1918 and How It Changed the World.* New York: Public Affairs, 2017.

Stoudt, Glenn. *The Selling of the Babe.* New York: Thomas Dunne Books, 2016.

Stump, Al. *Cobb: A Biography.* Chapel Hill, NC: Algonquin Books, 1994.

Surdam, David George, and Michael J. Haupert. *The Age of Ruth and Landis: The Economics of Baseball during the Roaring Twenties.* Lincoln: University of Nebraska Press, 2018.

Swift, Tom. *Chief Bender's Burden.* Lincoln: University of Nebraska Press, 2008.

Thomas, Henry W. *Walter Johnson: Baseball's Big Train.* Lincoln, NE: Bison Books, 1998.

Wagenheim, Kal. *Babe Ruth: His Life and Legend.* New York: Open Road, 2014.

Warren, Kenneth. *Bethlehem Steel: Builder and Arsenal of America.* Pittsburgh: University of Pittsburgh Press, 2008.

Waterman, Ty, and Mel Springer. *The Year the Red Sox Won the Series.* Boston: Northeastern University Press, 1999.

Wehrle, Edmund F. *Breaking Babe Ruth.* Columbia: University of Missouri Press, 2018.

Weingarden, Steve, and Bill Nowlin. *Baseball's Business: The Winter Meetings: 1901–1957.* Vol. 1. Phoenix, AZ: Society for American Baseball Research, 2016. Kindle edition.

Whalan, Mark. *American Culture in the 1910s.* Edinburgh: Edinburgh University Press, 2010.

Wiggins, Robert Peyton. *Chief Bender.* Jefferson, NC: McFarland, 2010.

Wills, Charles A. *Life and Times in 20th-Century America: Becoming a Modern Nation 1900–1920.* Vol. 1. Westport, CT: Greenwood Press, 2004.

Wood, Allen. *Babe Ruth and the 1918 Red Sox.* Bloomington, IN: iUniverse Star, 2000.

Wrinn, Daniel. *World War One: WWI History Told from the Trenches, Seas, Skies, and Desert of a War Torn World.* New York: Storyteller Books, 2021.

Ziegler, Robert H. *America's Great War.* Lanham, MD: Rowman and Littlefield, 2000.

Zoss, Joel, and John Bowman. *Diamonds in the Rough: The Untold History of Baseball.* Lincoln, NE: Bison Books, 2004.

INDEX

Page numbers in italics refer to illustrations.

William Ecenbarger, a freelance writer, is the author of *Pennsylvania Stories—Well Told* (Temple), *Walkin' the Line, Glory by the Wayside: The Old Churches of Hawaii*, and *Kids for Cash: Two Judges, Thousands of Children, and a $2.6 Million Kickback Scheme*. He is the coauthor of *Catching Lightning in a Bottle: How Merrill Lynch Revolutionized the Financial World* (with Winthrop H. Smith) and *Making Ideas Matter: My Life as a Policy Entrepreneur* (with Dwight Evans).